EYES OF A DIFFERENT COLOR

A MEMOIR OF LOVE FROM ISRAEL TO AMERICA

ROBERT JAFFEE, MD

PROLOGUE

I stand looking into a hole that will soon be the eternal resting place of a twenty-year old woman. A rabbi speaks in Hebrew, a language I don't understand. I assume it is a prayer for the dead. What good can it do? Will his prayer bring the dead to life? Will it make any sense of why I am here?

The sky is an endless blanket of sun this warm day in Israel. A mild breeze caresses the cemetery stones. I see a group of people in front of me, some known, some not. I don't feel the sun's warmth, I don't feel the breeze.

Oh, God, how did this happen? Make sense of this. I should not be here at this young woman's funeral. I should not be burying my wife.

CHAPTER ONE
The Introduction

Good morning Mrs. Schmidt. How can I help you?"

"Doctor, These glasses are just not right. I can't see with them," she said waving the glasses like a flag in front of me.

My examination noted that at age seventy-three Mrs. Schmidt was developing cataracts. I proceeded to see if a change in glasses' prescription would be of benefit.

"Now look at the eye chart and tell me which is clearer: choice one or choice two. Both may not be perfect, but which is better?" I said, placing two different lenses before her right eye. "Choice one or choice two?"

Mrs. Schmidt paused. "I don't like either. Nothing is clear."

"Neither may be perfect, but one will be better than the other. Just tell me which is better: one or two," I said again, alternating the lenses.

 Mrs. Schmidt responded instantly. "You're going too fast. They are not clear."

I felt I was speaking to her in a language she didn't understand. "Yes, I know they both may not be clear, but I need to know what direction to go in. I will go slower. Now, which is BETTER? BETTER, not great, but BETTER." I again put the lenses in front of her. "This is choice one, and this is choice two. Now which is clearer?"

Mrs. Schmidt's hands started to dance in her lap. "I don't like these choices. Don't you have a third choice?"

I looked down at the floor. The entire day had been like this. "Better one, or better two?" I had spent four years in medical school and completed a yearlong internship and three-year residency just to say, "better one or better two." I wanted to do surgery, see interesting medical cases, not just prescribe glasses. If I had known I only had to count to two to be an ophthalmologist, I could have gotten my medical degree in kindergarten.

I raised my voice. "No, I don't have a third choice. Which is BETTER, one or two, one or two? It is not difficult, really." Finally, after another fifteen minutes of "one or two" we arrived at the best possible prescription. Mrs. Schmidt looked down and shook her head. I took another twenty minutes to explain that cataracts were the cause of her visual decline and not the fault of the glasses. She shuffled out, head bowed, without making a return appointment.

With no other patient in the office, I was arranging the magazines in the waiting room when two women entered. I immediately recognized Lillie Karsai, wife of Karel Karsai, an ENT doctor. The noticeably young woman, or older girl, trailing behind Lillie I didn't recognize.

"Oh, look. Here he is," Lillie excitedly announced. "Dr. Bob, I want you to meet my beautiful niece, Iris. Iris, this is Dr. Bob, our fine new surgeon."

Several weeks earlier, Lillie had mentioned that her eighteen-year-old niece from Israel was coming to visit. Lillie had explained that she had just graduated from high school and would be on vacation before returning to Israel. She had asked if I might spend a little time showing the young woman around. I, a thirty-year-old single doctor, had just completed my residency in June, at New York University, and was starting my practice in ophthalmology. Most of my free time was occupied in preparation for my upcoming board exams in the subject, while working only two days a week in an office I shared with my ophthalmologist brother. I had completely forgotten about Lillie's niece.

We stood in the waiting room on the threadbare rugs. Iris rested her weight to one leg. Her long blond hair swung side to side like a clock pendulum as she looked at the water-stained ceiling and the faded bird pictures on the wall. Her face was light in tone with freckles. Tall, at about five feet nine, and slender, she wore tight jeans that accentuated her lean legs and shapely physique. Knowing what Lillie wanted from me and anxious to go to lunch, I got to the point.

"Glad to meet you. Lillie told me you were coming to the States. I don't know if you have any plans. There really isn't much to do here in Monticello. But if you like, I would be happy to take you to a movie on Saturday."

Iris looked at me, took a deep breath, and smiled faintly as "okay" dropped from her lips.

"I am sorry I don't have more time to chat, but I need to get lunch. I have another patient at one. A pleasure to meet you. I hope you enjoy your stay," I said, escorting Lillie and Iris out. I did not give a second thought to the introduction except to note that Iris was pretty, and I would be interrupting my studying by going to the movies.

* * *

Returning to the office after lunch, I waited for my one o'clock. I was surprised when the squeak of the door opening was not the entrance of my next patient but Lillie's niece—Iris, wasn't it?

"What happened to Lillie?"

"She go to bank. Will pick me when done," she said in an accent that was refreshing and kind of exotic compared to my New York one. She stood in front of me, straight as an arrow, looking directly into my eyes. Her young face hadn't a single blemish and her fair skin highlighted her blue eyes.

It was uncomfortable to be stared at—too intimate. I looked away and walked to the front door. "Come here. I'll show you something," I said, opening the door. "Monticello is not an attractive town, but it once was. You see the empty store across the street with the big Kaplan sign? It used to be a busy Jewish restaurant, what we call here a deli. Every Saturday night orthodox Jews lined up to enter. The smell of knishes and grilling franks filled the air. That vacant building next to it was a hardware store. I can remember coming here with my parents in the 1960s and admiring all the shiny new bikes lined up outside. Too bad—now, in 1979, it is empty. This was once a big resort area, where people came from New York City to vacation."

Iris looked up at me with a puzzled expression. "Why anyone want to come here? This place looks terrible."

I smiled in agreement. "Yeah, I guess it does look pretty bad." Closing the door, I turned toward her. "Let's go into my exam room and talk until my next patient arrives." I wasn't looking for a deep conversation, just some small talk until I went back to work. "How many weeks are you going to be here for?" I asked as we walked toward the back.

"I stay for eight weeks more."

"Will you be staying in Monticello the whole time?" I said as I pointed to the old wooden chair by the desk. "You can sit down if you want." She ignored the suggestion, so I sat behind the heavy, dark, wooden desk that, together with the chair, looked like a prop in a Norman Rockwell 1950s painting of a physician's office.

"I stay mostly here, but I want to take trip to California."

"What are you going to do when you go back to Israel?" I looked up at her while tapping my fingers on the desk.

Iris made a fist, dropping her chin as she whispered, "I go to army. All people eighteen have to go to army." It seemed like she had just gotten the death sentence of a convicted felon. She abruptly changed the subject "You like it here?" she said looking down at me.

"No, this place is awful," I loudly replied.

As though interrogating me for a crime, she continued staring directly into my brown eyes as I rose from my seat. "Why you stay here?" she said.

I felt this was getting too personal for someone I had just met, but it seemed she would not break her stare until I answered. "I'm passing time here, studying for my exams in ophthalmology in three months. When I finish those, I can decide if I want to stay here in practice with my brother or move on."

She seemed to be getting closer to me, not physically but by a deeper penetration of her gaze. "This place not nice. I would not stay here."

"Well, I am not sure I will stay here either, but it would be nice to work with my brother, as we are very close."

"Where you like to go?" Iris said, still looking into my eyes.

This was more of an examination than I was prepared for. The intercom rang. Perfect timing, I thought.

"Your next patient is here," my secretary announced.

"Well Iris, I guess it's time for me to go back to work." I left my desk and walked her out to the waiting room. She turned, facing me.

"You no forget Saturday," she commanded.

"No, I won't forget," I said with a grin as Iris turned away and sat down to await Lillie. I shrugged as I walked back to the exam room, feeling guilty about taking any time away from preparing for my upcoming exams.

Iris is young and pretty, but what could I have in common with a person from the other side of the world, a recent high-school graduate soon to enter the army?

I would fulfill Lillie's request and that would be the end, for me, of Iris.

As the patient entered the exam room, I took a deep breath, sat down, and went back to "better one, or better two."

CHAPTER TWO
The First Date

On Saturday evening I arrived at Lillie and Karel's townhouse to pick up Iris. Their house was spotless and smelled of paprika, a testament to their European roots. I took a seat on the sofa, which was so neat and clean it looked like a prop.

A framed photograph of Karel sat on the nearby table. Karel was tall, gruff, and husky with a deep, gravelly voice. He had done his medical training in Czechoslovakia before coming to the United States. I had visited my brother and him many times while training at NYU. He falsely presented himself as proud, uncompromising, taking no slights from anyone. But he was abused by the local physicians, who used him mostly for weekend emergencies while sending elective cases out of town.

I glimpsed at my watch and took a deep breath, noting Iris was late. Lillie saw my impatience.

"You know Israelis," Lillie said. "They can't be rushed. I think it is something we're born with, us Israelis."

Lillie, although born in Hungary, had survived Hitler's genocide and migrated to Israel before coming to the States. She considered herself European, Israeli, and American. I don't know how she met Karel or when they married. She was short and petite. Karel had a child from a previous marriage, in Europe, but Lillie was childless. One thing to know about Lillie, she was never one to keep her thoughts to herself. She had a good heart but could be overbearing.

Iris soon started down the stairs and paused on the landing to look at us. Wearing jeans that outlined a well-proportioned figure, a loose-fitting brown sweater and a scarf haphazardly wrapped around her neck, she looked stunning. Her hair carelessly swirled around her face, and she stood for a moment, relaxed in form, before continuing down the stairs. She gave me the impression of a woman with self-assurance and confidence much above her age.

Lillie spoke to her in Hebrew, and Iris replied in a harsh tone. Suddenly grabbing my arm, she said, "Let's go," and hurriedly pulled me toward the door.

"What were you and Lillie arguing about?" I asked as she dragged me out.

"She tell me what time to come back. She no let me do what I want. She should because I do it anyway. "What movie we go to." Iris said, releasing her grip on me.

"I don't know what is playing, so it will be a surprise to the both of us."

As we walked to the car, light shone from Lillie's living-room window when she parted the curtains to watch us leave. Iris walked once around my new red Datsun 280ZX sports car. It was the only expensive possession I owned, or almost owned considering the payments due on the loan. As we drove to the theater, I started to make light conversation by inquiring how Iris compared the United States to Israel.

Iris hesitated for a minute, trying to find the correct English words. "America very large. It have many things Israel not have as much of. Many things we wait long time for that you get now. You very rich country. Israel not so rich. It surprise me how much you drive; distances large. In Israel, everything much closer together, so we not drive much. Gas very expensive. Nobody able to afford big car like you have in States."

"Americans waste a lot of stuff. You must think us very greedy," I said, trying to sympathize with her.

She turned to me and said loudly, "Your country not always at war. Much money we spend to defend ourselves. If your country spent as much it not be able to have so many things."

It was time to lighten the conversation. "When I think of Israel, I imagine they still use camels to get around. Do you ride one?" I teased.

Iris turned toward me with a look of charity reserved for those too dumb to help themselves. "You really think we ride camels? Where you been in your life that you think country that fly jet plane in air ride camel on ground?"

I felt my conversational skills were quickly dying as I was being mocked by this eighteen-year-old. Fortunately, the conversation ended as we arrived at the small theater with a weathered marquee. The theater looked like its last picture had been a silent film from 1920. A faint light glowed around the half-missing letters spelling out the name of the movie. The movie was an action thriller—not my favorite genre—but it would suffice, especially since there was nothing else. We got some popcorn and soda and found our seats. The old velvet seats had many tears and our feet kept getting stuck on the gum covering the floors. The screen was small. Only a quarter of the theater was filled, mostly with older people, as few people in the twenty-to-forty age range lived in Monticello. There were no jobs in town to attract or retain younger residents.

The movie was filled with car chases and shoot-outs. I found it very boring, but Iris watched attentively. I was more interested in looking at Iris, who sexually aroused me. My male hormones were not satisfied by studying textbooks on ophthalmology.

The movie ended before my thought of putting my arm around her could occur.

Iris must have felt relieved to be away from Lille and Karel and be with someone a little closer to her in age and enjoying a night out. I couldn't think of any other reason she would hold on to my arm on the way back to the car. It was still early in the evening, and except for some dingy bars in town, there wasn't a place to go. I wanted a quiet place to talk. The place that came to mind was the local airport. I knew about the airport as I had a beginner pilot's license and had been to the airport before. At night, the airport had no lights and usually no planes coming or going. It was dark, desolate, and deserted. I parked the car, and we were alone. I told her how I rented a small plane there and practiced takeoffs and landings. My adventures included getting lost in Connecticut and winding up in Rhode Island. I really was a terrible pilot. She listened and laughed and never looked away. In the moonlight I kept looking into her face. I hadn't been with a woman for several months. I moved closer to her and put my arm around her shoulders.

"Iris, you are extremely attractive. Are all Israelis pretty like you?" I said as I was thinking what my next move would be.

She didn't move back but she didn't move closer either. I didn't know if she was purposely ignoring my question as she was still focused on my career. "Bob, if you no like Monticello, why you stay?" she asked quietly.

I felt guilty about seducing the girl and took my arm back and away from her. I stared at what facial features I could discern in the moonlight.

She just kept her eyes glued on me. "My stay in Monticello might only be temporary, until I take my board exams. I want to work with my brother. I have always looked up to him. But sometimes he's unfair. He has offered me several contracts to work with him which he later said he could not afford and reneged on the offer." I don't know why I was telling her all this. I guess it was a chance for me to release my own pent-up anger and bring out in words what I was thinking internally.

"Why you want to work with brother if you don't get along?" Iris asked, still looking intently at me.

It was a question I should have asked myself. I was beginning to think Iris was going to bill me for a psychology consult. But in that moment I wanted to forget my brother, my work, and my board exams. I was trying to forget everything, including why I was taking Iris out that evening. I again began to move closer to her.

"You're not really interested in hearing all the problems of an American doctor." I leaned over and kissed her. I was surprised when she leaned against me. We spent several minutes kissing and embracing. I unbuttoned her sweater and started to caress her breasts through her bra. She didn't resist. However, as much as I enjoyed the feel of her round, soft breasts, it just didn't seem right, a thirty-year-old physician seducing an eighteen-year-old girl entrusted to his care on vacation from a foreign country. I remembered Lillie looking out the window as we left. Somewhere in a corner of my brain was a shred of decency. I stopped and pulled away.

She was nonchalant. "You know, I like to kiss," she said buttoning her sweater.

I didn't know if she was serious or just wanted to show she was grown up. She certainly didn't seem angry.

"Look, I really enjoyed this evening, but I think we had better get back—it's getting late," I said. I did not want to do anything I would later regret. Neither of us commented on what had just happened. I didn't want her to think it was anything more than what it was, a man wanting sex. This was not going to be the beginning of a relationship for me. And what she thought she didn't say.

As we headed back to Lillie's I kept my conversation away from anything romantic. "Have you been to New York City?" I asked.

"No, but Lillie take me later in the week," Iris said.

I divided my attention between the road and occasional glimpses of Iris's face. "I'm sure you will like it. It is so exciting: the stores, the shows, and all. Just walking in the streets is fun. Watching the people, their dress and manners is fascinating. You'll find all the latest fashions. People there are from all over the world, every language, and every kind of person. I lived in Manhattan during my residency in New York. I could tell you stories about the city, about the disco nightclubs, which were big when I lived there. It is just so different from any place you have probably been to."

Iris smiled. "You been to many places?"

"Not exactly, but I have lived in several places. Med school in Wisconsin, interned in Pittsburgh, lived in Connecticut and Maine and New York City before coming to Monticello. That doesn't qualify me as a world traveler, but I've been around."

"I been to Italy, Holland, and France. I love to travel," Iris responded.

I felt chagrined. "I've been to Gettysburg. I bet you've never been there."

A quizzical expression came upon her face. "Gettysburg? Where's that?"

We arrived at Lillie's. I was glad I didn't have to answer and admit that my "world" travels were limited to the States. Gettysburg sounded French to me. I thought she would think it some exotic place, instead of what it is, a Civil War battlefield in Pennsylvania.

"Well, here we are. I had a great evening." I leaned over and gave Iris a kiss on the cheek. Now that Lillie's request had been fulfilled, Iris would soon fade from my memory. I rationalized to myself that my actions this evening were just impulse and that I had stopped before I went too far.

Iris opened the passenger-side door and climbed out. "Tomorrow maybe you come over for lunch?"

I was surprised and tried to think of a reason to say no. I told myself seeing her would lead nowhere, just a waste of time. "I'm very busy studying for my exams in the morning, and I work in the afternoons."

"That no excuse. You find time, you eat lunch, right? So, you come. Okay?" Iris said, putting her hands on her hips and raising her voice.

I honestly don't know why, maybe because she was so adamant, I smiled and answered: "Yes, I'll be there at noon."

She turned, walked to Lillie's door, and paused on the steps to watch me drive off.

Oh well, Iris is easy on the eyes, a good listener, and interesting. A little time away from studying wouldn't hurt. And I do need to eat lunch.

CHAPTER THREE
Lunch

*H*ave you got a menu, or can I order anything I want?" I said with a smirk as I arrived for lunch the following day. Iris and I were alone in the Karsais' kitchen. Karel and Lillie, who was Karel's secretary, had gone to work at the office building (a converted house) owned by my brother.

"How about eggs?" Iris replied as if the menu was a fait accompli. "I make good eggs."

"For lunch? Who eats eggs for lunch?"

I stood facing Iris as she exhaled, placed her hands on her hips, and looked directly at me. "We do in Israel. You think maybe you die if you eat eggs for lunch?"

"No, I don't think I will die, but maybe you have something else.

Let's look in the refrigerator." I brushed past Iris, walked over to the refrigerator, opened the door, and peered inside.

Iris slapped her hands to her sides, turned toward me and confessed: "I don't know how to make anything else."

I realized I was being a jerk. Here was this young woman trying to be nice, and I was acting like I was ordering from a restaurant. I still didn't want eggs for lunch. I answered in a soft voice: "Oh, great. We have some cooked chicken. We can make some sandwiches."

"What is a sandwich?" she asked, her breath warm on my neck.

"You don't know what a sandwich is?" I said as I straightened up and turned to face her. "Here, I'll show you. You take two pieces of bread. You know what bread is," I teased.

"Shut up!" She scowled.

"You place meat on a slice of bread and spread this white sauce called mayonnaise on the top piece of bread. Then you put them together and make a sandwich. Got it?" I said triumphantly, holding the prize in front of her on a plate.

She turned a mild shade of red and gave out a huff. "Okay, you sit down. I do the rest. If a stupid American can do it, no problem for an Israeli." She grabbed the plate, carried it to the dining room, and banged it on the table, then returned to the kitchen to make a sandwich for herself.

I couldn't stop teasing. "How is it that you never learned to cook? Don't people eat in Israel?"

There was fire in Iris's eyes as she brought her sandwich to the table. I thought she might ignite the Karsais' town house. "My mother do all the cooking in our house so I no learn to cook. If you no like it, you no have to eat what I make."

I managed to keep my sarcasm to myself, even when Iris could not make a cup of instant coffee, as nobody in her family drank coffee. It probably would have been easier to have just gone out for lunch. But finally, with some added help, lunch was ready.

While we ate, she asked me about my plans, and again I complained about how boring work was and how I didn't know where I would go after my exams.

"It not always have to be like this," she said, leaning toward me with sympathy in her voice. "If you good, then someday, you go to better place and be something."

I laughed as I got up to leave. "By that time, I'll probably be too old to work. Anyhow, I'd better go back to the office. It was fun." I downed my last bite of sandwich and walked to the door, Iris following me out. At the door she took me by surprise by kissing me on the cheek.

"It okay if I come later to see you work?" she said, smiling as I turned back.

I wasn't sure why she wanted to see me again. And I certainly didn't know why she kissed me. I spent lunch mocking her.

She must really be bored! I thought.

But I had to admit being with her was fun. She didn't wilt from my ridicule, and she seemed interested in my troubles. "Yes, if you want. You'll have the opportunity to see one of the world's greatest ophthalmologists perform miracles."

I could hear her laughter as she closed the door behind me.

CHAPTER FOUR
A Bad Joke

*A*fternoon at work progressed as usual: two people with nothing wrong wanting to chat; three people who needed new glasses to see; three people who needed new glasses to appease their minds; and one person looking for a chiropractor who'd found me by mistake. After I had finished with my last patient for the day and was cleaning up the exam room, I heard the front door open and footsteps approach. From the sound, I knew it was my brother, Steven. I wondered why he'd come, as it was my afternoon to work.

"Bob, you done already?"

"Yeah, not much going on. Did you forget something?" I said.

Steven rubbed his hands together, and small beads of sweat appeared on his forehead as he spoke. "When we thought about working together, I thought there would be enough business for the both of us, but it hasn't turned out that way."

Knowing Steven, this was a prelude to a sermon.

"This place is really dying. Things are tight, and expenses high. You believed you would just start working, and patients would be waiting for you."

I'd never thought that patients would just turn up without any effort on my part, but my brother had always thought himself an older, wiser sage, so I let him continue. It was useless to try to stop him.

"Not so easy to start a practice. You are getting a real education in business here. I think it's only fair that for any patient who comes to you for surgery, I get half," Steven said.

I would have thought it a poor joke, but his demeanor left little doubt about his seriousness.

"Now, before you complain, just listen. Any surgical cases you do are cases I would be doing if you weren't here. People are coming here because of my reputation, not yours. Therefore, I feel I should be compensated for losing cases to you," he went on.

I became aware of my tightly clenched fists. "You mean to tell me that if I examine a patient and decide they need surgery, do the surgery, take the responsibility, and do the follow-up, I'm supposed to give you half the money? Are you crazy?" I shouted.

"Look, patients are not coming here to see you. You're taking the bread out of my mouth when you do surgical cases I could be doing."

Not many surgeries were performed in Monticello, as most patients didn't trust a doctor in a small town. They ran off to New York City for their surgery. But surgeries did pay well. I was in disbelief; this was surely a nightmare. "Why the hell didn't you tell me this before I came here to work? If I'd known you were going to rob me blind, I would have looked for somewhere else to practice," I said loudly.

"Don't blame me. I told you to look around, to see what was available, before coming here. Your expectations would have been more reasonable."

Although I was only initially to stay in Monticello until my exams were finished, my brother and I had talked at length about working together. I was under the impression this was the goal for both of us. I couldn't hide my disgust. "You're such a damn money monger that you'd cheat your own brother. I can't believe you're serious. Look, I'll tell you what. Don't do me any favors. Keep all the money, that way you can sleep at night."

Steven strode out of the exam room toward the front area. "Don't be stupid. I don't want all the money. Think about it for a while. I'm going to the grocery store. I'll meet you at home."

"I don't need to think about it. It stinks!" I yelled, following him.

He left, and I just stood in the entry, shoulders slumped, shaking my head. I didn't know how to reply further or what to do. It was July 1979. I had only been in Monticello for a month. Now I had not only my exams to worry about but the necessity of finding a decent place to work when the exams were finished. This placed extra importance on passing the boards because it would be exceedingly difficult to find a position if I flunked.

I turned back to the waiting room and found Iris sitting alone. I hadn't noticed her among the fury of our conversation. She must have been sitting there long enough to hear the argument.

"You finished?" she asked.

A faint grin came across my face. "You might say I'm finished." I headed back toward the examination room. "Well, come on in. Your sitting in the waiting room makes it look like a crowd has formed."

She looked around the room. "But nobody else here."

"Iris, in my waiting room, you only need one person to be a crowd."

"It sounds like you and your brother have a fight," she said, trailing behind me.

Suddenly I wanted to get out of the office to cool off. There was no one waiting, and the appointment book was empty. "Come on, let's get out of here," I said as I grabbed her hand and exited the building with her in tow. I locked the front door, and we started strolling up Monticello's Broadway. In silence we passed the empty stores only occupied by the homeless who camped in the entry. I didn't say anything. I could focus only on what had just happened and what I would do in the future.

After a minute of silence, Iris halted. I turned toward her but before I could say a word, she looked directly at me. "What happen with you and brother?"

We stood on the sidewalk as I explained to her what had just occurred. I asked her if she had similar family problems.

"Me and family not in business together. We get along very well. I have fights with my father, but usually I win."

"Don't you listen to your father?"

Iris started to smile. "Oh, I listen, but I don't do what he say all the time. My mother and I get along great. She and I very close on everything. My father one of nicest man in world, but my mother and I, how you say, see things as one. Maybe you say eye to eye."

"Yes, you got it right. It sounds like you and your family really get along."

Iris widened her smile, looking away from me as we again started to walk along the street. "Yes, me and my sister, Alina, also talk a lot. She ask me advice on boyfriends. She so pretty, much prettier than I am. And my youngest sister, Noah, so sweet. I miss her."

When I asked the ages of her sisters, I was surprised that Alina was thirteen and Noah one.

"Noah just happened; it was not on purpose. I guess Noah an accident, but we very happy to have her. I can't wait to see her again." She was looking off in the distance, still with a wide grin, as if she could visualize herself back home with her sisters. She seemed so calm and content, just beaming with pride.

"I envy you," I said. "The way you talk about your family shows so much love. It surprises me that you left them to come to the States."

"It very important to me to see the world before army. I miss family, but I go back."

We walked for about an hour, and as it was getting late in the afternoon, we headed back to the office. Although I had felt my stomach in knots and a little nauseous after the fight with my brother, Iris's composure seemed contagious. She was so content with her life, loved her family, loved to travel. Being with her had a calming effect on me.

Steven, his wife, Nancy, and I went, occasionally, to auctions for some diversion on weekends. It was a cheap way to spend a day if you kept your wallet in your pocket. I didn't know if Steven and I would be talking after our disagreement but, now feeling less angry, I thought I would like to go on one of these outings. I had only known Iris for a few days, but I enjoyed being with her. She could listen, she could advise, she could laugh, and she could feel.

As I drove Iris back to Lillie's, I asked her if she would come to the auction.

"I would love to come," she said, lightly taking hold of my arm and turning toward me. "What is an auction?"

I took my eyes away from the road and looked at her. "How do you know you want to go if you don't even know what an auction is?"

I could see a smile arising across her freckles. "Well, you will be there, you pay for gas, and you buy lunch, so it all good."

Now we were both smiling.

27

CHAPTER FIVE
The Auction

*U*pon returning home to Steven's house that evening, I went to my room to resume studying. Steven entered, momentarily interrupting me. We avoided further discussion over sharing surgical fees.

"Are we still going to the auction this weekend?" I asked. "I would like to invite Iris."

"Yeah, if you want. I have no objections to taking Iris. What's she like?" Steven said.

"Oh, she's kind of nice. A little shy, she's pretty but a little young."

"Afraid you'll end up in jail?" Steven replied, smiling.

Iris seemed so mature that I forgot she was only eighteen. "Not funny. Anyhow she is eighteen and legal. Now, get out of my room. I've got to study before dinner." I said, turning away from Steven.

"Don't wear out your brain," Steven teased as he left. "Just remember, they can't flunk everyone. You're bound to have some chance of passing, even if you're an idiot."

Very encouraging.

* * *

The auction house was in a small, picturesque town by a river, an hour's drive from Monticello. The auction house itself was nothing fancy. It was a large one-story building with rows of folding chairs in the center for the participants. In the front, by the auctioneer's lectern, and along the sides was the merchandise to be auctioned, each with a number corresponding to the order to be sold and description in the printed catalog. It was mostly a lot of not-so-old furniture, glassware, lamps, and dishes. It looked like stuff expelled from a recent house cleaning. Iris and I took a quick look and realized neither one of us had any interest in the items for sale.

"Iris let's go for a walk and leave the capitalists behind," I suggested. Iris nodded approvingly.

We left Steven and Nancy at the auction and headed out for a walk. There was a path along the river, and it was a beautiful day in July with a mild breeze. I again asked about her future.

"What will happen when you go back home?"

"I go to army. All people aged eighteen go to army. I not want to go. I hate it!"

I had never served in the army. I didn't know a thing about army life. "How do you know you will hate it? You haven't gotten there. Besides, it will give you a chance to grow up."

Iris snorted, stopped and looked at me. "What do you mean grow up? You think I baby now?"

"Well, no, but you've always lived at home and you're just out of high school. Being in the military will give you a chance to meet other people, form new experiences."

"It's a waste of time. You ever been in army?" She was looking at me with such intensity that I knew I had hit a sore subject.

"No, I was deferred for medical school," I said.

Iris was quick to pounce, her voice soaring in mockery. "You some hero. You go to army; then you talk to me."

"Can you get out of the army?"

"If I marry, I no have to go. But I not marry till I twenty-seven," she said turning away from me as she resumed walking.

"Twenty-seven?" I laughed as I followed her. "I'm glad you've thought this out. Anything special about twenty-seven? Are twenty-six and twenty-eight out of the question?"

Iris's lips curved in a half smile. "No. Twenty-seven," she insisted.

I continued to laugh at her prophecy. "Yes, twenty-seven is a good age. I passed through it once but forgot to get married. I suppose you'll have your first child at twenty-eight and a half."

"Twenty-nine," Iris said, smiling from ear to ear.

"Of course. I should have suspected. Tell me, if you find someone you want to marry at age twenty-two, what will you do?"

"He wait," she said without hesitation. "How come you not married?"

Taking a pause before answering as we continued walking, "I was almost married twice, but it just wasn't right."

She stopped and looked again directly into my eyes. She had done this several times before and I felt like she was discovering, each time, something inside of me that I wanted to hide.

"The first time, I was just too young. I was still in medical school. I had dated the girl for two years. She was nice and all, but I just didn't feel I could stay married to her."

Iris just kept staring at me. I realized the explanation was incomplete.

"I was a kid. I'd gone out with maybe two girls before I met her. I had years of training still before me—hard years. She was also the same age as me. I felt I could not remain faithful to her under those conditions. I would want to go out with other younger women when I had the time and opportunity. Unfortunately, a woman's biological clock ticks faster than a man's. Selfish, yes, but that is what I thought would happen."

Iris was not done with the interrogation. "And the second woman?"

"The second girl was exceptionally beautiful. It took me a year to realize I was mostly in love with her looks. In the end I felt she really didn't love me either. I also didn't want children right away, and she did. I thought a marriage should grow first. The couple should make sure they get along before starting a family." It was my time to interrogate her. "And what about you? No lovers? No one you'd thought to run away with?"

Iris pulled some wayward strands of hair away from her face. "I had boyfriend in Holland. He want to come to Israel, but never arrive. I meet him last year when I travel in Europe."

"How long did you know him for?" *Was this some torrid love affair?*

"I in Holland about two weeks."

"Two weeks, and you loved him? How could you know in two weeks?" I shrieked.

Iris calmly responded as if the answer was self-evident. "Oh, you can feel when it right. But this not very serious. He just friend."

We had been walking for a while, and I thought it was time to return. I laughed to myself that Iris, at eighteen, had already decided when to marry, when to have kids, and to hate the army. This was probably just immature youth speaking. But she was good company and great looking. If not for the fact that she was Lillie's niece, I would certainly try to be more intimate.

I stopped walking, and as I looked at her, I forgot about Lillie. "Iris, have you decided when you're going to New York City?"

"I go later with Lillie, but she will take me around and lead me. I don't have good time as if on my own."

This was the perfect opening for me. "Why don't you go with me to the city? As I mentioned before, I lived there for two years and know some of the good places to see." I tried to make it sound inviting. "There are great restaurants, great shopping. We could get tickets to a Broadway play. We could have a fun time spending a night there. Do you think you would like to go?" I said excitedly.

Without hesitation Iris grabbed my arm. "Yes, I want to go. I think it much more fun with you than Lillie. But I do not think Lillie will like it very much. Maybe I not tell her."

I chuckled. "It's going to be hard to disappear for two days without telling her." I knew Lillie was not going to be happy with me taking her niece on an overnight trip to New York City, but the worst she could do was say no. "Let's plan to go next weekend. If something comes up and you can't make it, let me know."

Iris's eyes sparkled with excitement. "Okay."

I was glad and a little surprised to see her so enthusiastic. "I'll get tickets for a Broadway show, a musical, if I can. I think you will really like that."

We arrived back at the auction house as the auction was ending. Steven and Nancy had not bought anything, and Steven looked bored. He took a deep breath as if inflating himself. "There is nothing I want, and besides, I've got to preserve money if I'm going to pay the heating bills for my cold brother."

I knew Steven was kidding. I turned to Iris. "Listen to him. I pay him for room and board so that he can attempt to freeze me out. It's so cold in his house that in winter I climb into the refrigerator to keep warm. There's no hot water. You must take a shower in a coat."

Steven shook his head, as he always had to have the last word. He and Nancy rose from their seats. "Okay, okay, Iris got the point. Look at him, Iris. Does he look underfed? Does he look sickly? I ask you—does he look abused?" he said.

Iris, not sure what to say, just shrugged as Steven continued: "However, if he doesn't shut up, he's going to look dead." And with that we got into the car and headed back to Monticello.

On the way back I thought how Iris and I would be sharing a room in New York City. I didn't think I was taking advantage of her; I figured she must know that if she is spending the night with me, it is not in a separate room. She was willing and of legal age. I didn't think either one of us would take this as anything more than an enjoyable weekend.

How could this be anything more? She's going back to Israel in six weeks. This could not be an opportunity for a long-lasting relationship, just a fun time for both of us.

he had been too generous and had to reduce my benefits. Nancy would never disagree with Steven in public.

I wanted to leave this environment as soon as possible, if only for a couple of days. I went back to my room and finished packing my suitcase. As I walked past Steven, he momentarily glanced up from the table as he finished his dessert. Nancy said nothing as she continued cleaning the dishes.

"Son of a bitch," I whispered to myself, slamming the door behind me.

* * *

I did not want to face Lillie to explain why I was taking her niece on an overnight trip to New York City. When I arrived to pick up Iris, I just honked my horn. Then I honked it again several more times. I looked anxiously, in the dark, at the front door.

Could she have changed her mind?

The drapes of the window parted, and I could see Iris looking out. She saw my red car and gave me a hand sign she would be out momentarily. The front door opened, and she flew out carrying a small suitcase as if running from a fire. Before I could get out of the car, she opened the door, threw her luggage in the back, got in, and put her arms around my neck, kissing me on the lips.

"I so excited," she said.

I felt she must really be glad to get away from Monticello and be going to Manhattan. After all it couldn't be me that was so exciting.

"Yes, we will have a great time. But if you don't let go of me, we will never get there," I said with a smile. She gave a huff, put on her seat belt, and we were off. I still had the argument with Steven ringing in my ears and as we drove, I explained what had just occurred.

"Why you not out on own?" she said, turning to me in the car.

"It's not so easy. It takes lots of money to open an office, money that I don't have. I just finished my residency and bought this car. I would have to borrow money to start a practice and it would take tens of thousands of dollars."

Iris thought for a second. "You not happy with brother. You need to have life of own."

Growing up, my brother and I had been close. He was supportive of me. He would defend me against bullies and encouraged me to stay in medical school when I wanted to quit. He inspired me to consider ophthalmology as a career.

"I can't believe our differences will keep us apart," I said. "Steven is not as bad as I am telling you. He's a good doc. But he likes to feel he is always right, which is kind of annoying."

"You wrong if think brother will change. If you not happy, then you need to change. If you wait, then only more bad times to come. If you stay, you always be little doctor, and he always be big doctor giving you orders."

Although I saw the wisdom of her statement, I wasn't ready to give up all hope of working with Steven. He was always the older, wiser brother who had given me advice. I had always looked up to him. We had disagreements, sure, all brothers do. But no decision needed to be made immediately.

What was immediate was the skyline of Manhattan, which we were soon approaching.

We arrived in the city at 11:00 p.m. Our hotel was in the lower part of Manhattan near Lexington Avenue. It was a commercial area of the city and not very populated after 5:00 p.m. The hotel was cheap and looked it. But with the cost of a play and dining, it was all that I could afford, and at 11:00 p.m., it was too late to look for something else. The only thing that sparkled in the building was the cheap jewelry on the hookers who decorated the lobby. I had placed my precious car in a nearby parking lot and prayed it would be safe. We registered as Mr. and Mrs. Smith—probably not the first time the clerk had seen this. The tiny elevator took us to a room that looked smaller than our suitcases. The bed took up most of the room, and in this hotel, was probably the only thing needed. The wallpaper was dirty and torn. I was embarrassed, but I rationalized we would be spending most of our time out of the room. Iris looked around but said nothing. Maybe she had seen hotels like this while traveling in Europe. Maybe she was too young to realize how cheap this hotel was. Or maybe she was just being polite.

"I want to go for a walk," Iris said as we unpacked.

"It's late and there's nobody on the streets. I don't think it's safe."

"It will be fine, I've got you," she said as she embraced me.

I looked at her and protested once more, but she was adamant. I didn't want to disappoint her. Ignoring my better judgment, I gave in. It is hard to turn down a beautiful woman's request while she's kissing you.

The July night was humid, but there was a touch of an inviting breeze. We ran down the street as the wind carried dust and small debris around us. Iris was delighted by the vastness of it all, the never-ending buildings that looked, in the dim streetlights, like vertical French Fries. I tried to paint a mental picture of the crowds and noise that would, in the morning, fill the space. Her eyes shone as if they had discovered the storeroom of her dreams. She didn't want to go back to the hotel, but it was late, and we had wandered some distance. I broke the spell and we returned.

Back at the hotel we laid back on the one bed and discussed our itinerary for the next day. Iris didn't mention what I thought she must have known was coming. Her white slacks hugged her slim figure; the cloth outlined the curves of a youthful body. I was excited to see her undressed. Kissing her on the forehead, I pushed aside her long hair, exposing her neck. I started to kiss her ear and moved to kiss her cheek and neck. My hands settled on her back, then moved forward to her breasts. I stopped to feel and gently squeezed them through her top. Iris just held on to my back. I proceeded to rub her breasts gently, very gently. My left hand slipped down to the edge of her shirt. Fingers slipped beneath the shirt to touch her flat stomach. Iris still did not move, did not say a word. She just buried her head against my shoulder. I unclasped her bra. I pressed my left hand against an erect breast, compressing the soft, warm mass. With my right hand I lifted her top over her head and off. Her bra fell away, and now I could see her pink, youthful breasts. With my mouth, I started engaging her right breast. I outlined her nipple with my tongue as I slid my right hand down her back to her round bottom. I felt her buttocks through her jeans as a blind man would feel braille, touching carefully and fully so as not to miss a sensation imprinted on my hand. My fingers found her pants button and released it. I relaxed for a minute, pulling my head back while my hand traveled over her. I felt her breasts, her well-shaped bottom, the tightness of her long calves, putting together in my mind her naked figure before I saw the final vision. Her pants yielded as I again slipped my palm onto her buttocks. Her flesh was delightful to the touch: soft like fur, smooth like glass.

I could barely control my excitement; but Iris's restraint was the antithesis of my fervor. She did not push my hands away, but she had no passion. She just was there, like a bowl of soup being devoured by a hungry man. When I started to ease her pants off, she asked that I turn off the one working light, leaving only enough streetlight to shadow her form. I grabbed the legs of her pants and pulled them off. Nude except for her panties, she rolled over and pulled the blankets across her.

I took from my pants pocket a condom that I had placed in advance, hoping for this opportunity. After undressing myself, I climbed beneath the sheets beside her. I rolled on top of her, my left hand beneath her panties, caressing her.

As I was unwrapping the condom Iris said I didn't need one as she was taking birth control pills. She stared up at the ceiling. She looked so innocent, stiff and uninterested. But if she was on the pill, she must have had prior sex, I thought. I asked her if she was a virgin.

"That something you don't need to know," she said defiantly.

There was no sensual response from her. She stayed still and calm as if waiting patiently for a train to arrive.

"Iris, is anything wrong?" I said.

She shrugged and turned to her side.

"Am I hurting you?"

"No," she said quietly. "You can continue."

I was losing interest. There was no passion or spontaneity from her. She acted as though she had an obligation to fulfill: a thank-you for taking her to Manhattan. I did not want to make love to a cadaver. She was obviously not ready for this. Although I could have forced myself upon her, I liked her too much to make her feel uncomfortable. It was time to remind myself that I was thirty and she was only eighteen. No matter what I desired, the appropriate action was to stop. I put my arm around her and kissed her on the cheek. She nestled her head into my chest. We held each other until we were asleep among the blaring car horns and distant shouts coming from the street.

CHAPTER SEVEN
Manhattan

The next morning, rain clouds threatened. We had to dress carefully in the small room so as not to bump into each other.

"Iris, what do you want for breakfast?"

"Some tahini, salad, and pita."

"Tahini? What the hell is that?"

Iris rolled her eyes. "Just because you not smart enough to know what tahini is, don't laugh at me. It very good. It a white sauce you put on bread to make it taste better. Maybe I have some fish for breakfast too."

"Salad and fish?" I said laughing. "Lady, this is America. You need an American breakfast: eggs, bacon, and pancakes."

"Why you eat so much in the morning? It make me tired if I eat so much. I watch you eat."

"Oh, no. We will both eat. I don't want to be the only one falling asleep from a big breakfast," I said, taking her by the hand as we left the room.

We found a diner conveniently located across from the hotel. Being the business district, it was crowded with people grabbing a bite before work. It was a typical city diner: small, with booths along the wall and windows, aisles so narrow we had to walk sideways. The maître d/cashier/busboy pointed to a vinyl upholstered booth for us. Nothing fancy in the plain Formica tables without tablecloths, cutlery so heavy you could use it to chop wood. The plastic laminate menus stained with assorted blobs of butter and jelly gave silent testimony to heavy morning use. Smells of sizzling beacon and brewing coffee filled the air along with the chatter of busy New Yorkers.

Iris took a confused look at the menu. After I decided on my selection, I looked to her.

"I don't understand anything," she said with a huff. "You order for me. If I don't like, then you eat it."

I ordered for her what I thought was a safe American breakfast of pancakes. She pecked at it like it was some dangerous object, took two bites, a sip of coffee, and was done. Eating my breakfast and her remains, I knew she was right. I was tired. We—or rather, I—finished breakfast and paid the bill, and we were on our way uptown.

"How far we have to walk?" Iris said as we walked briskly along Madison Avenue.

It was a lovely day, in the seventies with clouds but no rain, a good day to walk. "A couple of miles. It's good for you," I said, laughing. "It will get you ready for the army."

Iris did not laugh. "I hate to walk. You keep walking this fast and you walk alone."

I turned to see her dragging along. "The Israeli army is going to be in big trouble when you arrive. I hope they win all their wars before you get home."

She frowned. "Not funny. We Israelis not like all of you Americans. You talk a lot but don't do much."

I slowed my steps so she could catch up. We were soon even in stride. The tall skyscrapers seemed to tickle heaven as they peered down on us. Taxis honked at anything in their way. Pedestrians dodged each other and the traffic. Everybody rushed as if they were forty minutes late to wherever they were going.

"We in Israel die for our country," Iris said. "You American Jews come to Israel to spend money and have good time. If you people so concerned about Israel, why don't you not go live there? Why you not give up big house and car to live in Israel?"

I quit mocking her and became serious. "Although there are many Jews in the US, and Israel may be their spiritual home, the US is where they were born."

"But Israel place where all Jews can come to live. It only safe place in world where Jews who have no other place to go can come."

"Israel is little. The United States gives Israel a lot of money. How long do you think Israel would last without this help?" I said.

"But you give money, we give blood."

"And what if all the Jews in the world went to Israel? It is unfortunate that your people must fight, but if not for Jews in other places helping to get support for Israel, then Israel would not exist. If all the Jews in the world lived in Israel, then you would have a ghetto, and I know you learned what happened to the ghettos of Poland and Russia. It is better that we Jews are all over the globe. When some of us are killed, there are still some who remain alive."

She looked around at all the affluence of Manhattan, at the filled store windows, at the well-dressed citizens going about their lives. I felt she was expressing some pent-up resentment about returning home to be in the army.

"I no want to talk about it anymore. It make me angry," she said.

I was glad we were done with the topic, as neither of us was selling their opinion to the other. We continued walking up Madison Avenue. The shadows of the tall skyscrapers like long arms enveloping us. Stopping at a jewelry store to gawk, Iris peered at the showcases of expensive trinkets.

"Which do you like?" she asked, looking at the watches.

"Let's see if we agree. You pick out a watch you like, and I'll pick one I like," I said.

Iris chose a simple watch. Simple gold, simple diamond numerals. It was not ostentatious or gawdy, but commanded attention because of its obvious quality. Wanting to see what her expression would be, I picked out a watch with rubies, diamonds, and emeralds. It looked like something I could use in my office to test for color blindness. It was ugly, but I wanted to see her reaction.

Her eyes sprang open as she shook her head. "You crazy? That awful looking. You not know what good."

"What makes you so sure you know what is good?" I asked.

"It no take a lot of brain to see that what you pick is ugly. If something nice, it no have to yell at you. Come, you waste time here," she said. I smiled. I didn't want to let her know I agreed with everything she said. She took my arm, and we were back on Madison.

We went in and out of shops like crocheting needles. It was fun admiring the toys of the rich. It was fun seeing the diversity of the people walking along the streets, including the person holding up a sign proposing to relieve one of any demons they had. Suddenly a shriek arose from Iris.

"Bob, Bob! Oh, we must stop," she squealed, her sight laser-focused on the counter of a falafel stand.

I had been around New York City for years and didn't know what falafel was, much less—until now—where to get it. She grabbed my arm as we ran to the stand.

"What is a falafel?" I asked.

Her eyes widened as she hurriedly exclaimed. "It something we eat all the time in Israel. Like you eat hamburger, we eat falafel. It Arab food. It got lettuce, cooked round balls, and tahini."

Iris took control ordering for the both of us. I was going to have my first falafel. She spoke a few words of Hebrew to the cook. They laughed, gesticulated with flying hands, grimaced, contorted their faces, shrugged. It looked like two mimes communicating. When all was done, we had a couple of pockets of bread with some round fried things and a lot of vegetables swimming in a sea of thin white sauce bleeding out.

When I took a bite, the white sauce exsanguinated all over my clothes. "This is a mess; it tastes good, but it's a real mess."

Iris was obviously more practiced in the art of eating falafel, as she avoided getting even one drop of sauce on her. She looked over at me and started to laugh at my ineptness. "No, it's not a mess. You just klutz."

We were both laughing as I cleaned myself off with a series of napkins. Arm in arm, like an old married couple we walked to Broadway to pick up the tickets I had reserved, stopping occasionally to peer into the shop windows before arriving at the theater.

* * *

If one has never seen a Broadway play, it is impressive, and this was a first for Iris. The play was "I Remember Mama" at the Majestic Theater. It had been panned in review but was the only musical I could get tickets for at such short notice. Our seats were in the balcony. We were enclosed by walls with arched panels and motifs of leaves and flowers. They were flanked by pilasters topped by urns and caryatids. Brass sconces on the wall and chandeliers hanging from the terracotta ceiling gave off a subdued yellowish light. When the lights dimmed, the music played, and the stage curtains parted you were transported to a world far from the mundane, even if the play was tiresome. During intermission she buoyantly gave her opinion in an increasingly loud voice. "It very nice. So much music, and so many actors." Continuing in a more subdued tone, "I want to be an actor or director when I done with army. You know, I study ballet when I in high school. I very good but not much opportunity with ballet in Israel. Maybe there be job in acting."

I didn't think that Israel had many opportunities for acting. Her declaration sounded immature, the dreams of a young girl, but I didn't want to dampen her enthusiasm with reality—or that is, reality as I saw it. It was too bad she was going back to Israel in a few weeks and this entire interlude would be ending shortly. I did wish she was an American and I could continue seeing her; we were having such an enjoyable time together.

When the show ended, it was time to return to the hotel, retrieve our suitcases, and head back to Monticello. We flagged a taxi. On the way back I pointed out some Hasidic Jews in their traditional black clothing.

"You must have a lot of religious people like that in Israel," I said.

"We have some people like that, but not most. They very religious and we not get along with them so good. They crazy!"

"What do you mean, they're crazy?"

Iris appeared bored, as if the answer was self-evident. "These people are very few, maybe ten percent of the country, but because of government, they get most of their way. They very religious. To stay in power, the prime minister need them, so he do what they want. To keep them happy, they get laws that most of country not want."

"Wait, you mean you're not religious?" I said, raising my eyebrows.

Iris smiled. "I not religious even a little. My father go to pray on high holy days and he fast, but my mother and me never go to temple and don't fast."

I was surprised at this response, as I assumed all Jews in Israel were somewhat religious. "Why, even I fast on Yum Kippur, and I didn't think it possible to be less religious than me and still be Jewish."

Iris shook her head. "In Israel, I no have to prove I'm Jewish. Everyone Jewish. I live in a Jewish state. I Jewish, but I no believe in praying. I no have to follow things I not believe in to be a Jew."

I had a different opinion. "I have lived in different parts of this country where there weren't many Jews. If you didn't want to get lost in the majority, you had to keep some customs and go to temple; otherwise, you would soon forget you were Jewish. Even though, like you, I don't believe in most of the religious laws, I still went to temple just to feel that I belonged."

Iris hesitated before answering. Her eyes widened and her face became taut. "It no make sense to me to go to something I don't believe in. It false."

The taxi pulled in front of the hotel, and our discussion ended. We were ecstatic that our suitcases hadn't been stolen. I was doubly ecstatic that my car was present and undamaged. We got in and headed back to Monticello.

Could a relationship possibly develop between a soon-to-be-unemployed ophthalmologist and a teenager who lives six thousand miles away? No, no, it would be impossible.

CHAPTER EIGHT
California and Back

I don't know if I want to go or not," Iris said about her upcoming trip to California over lunch at the local diner. "I meet Israeli man in the American Embassy when I go to get passport. We talk about going to California together to cut down cost."

"Is he someone your parents know?" I asked.

"No, I just meet him this time and one other time. But he seem very nice. It very common for people in Israel to travel together with people they just met."

Ted Bundy *seemed* nice too. This was a very foolish and potentially dangerous idea. "I don't understand how you can trust people so easily," I said shaking my head in disbelief.

Her plans were to leave the following week, although she had misgivings. We did not discuss it further.

I was surprised when only two days into her trip Lillie told me at the office that Iris was returning. I was curious as to the reason for her early return.

"I don't know. She didn't say, but you know I wouldn't be surprised if it was because of you. She really likes you. Maybe she just misses you too much." Lillie said.

She was returning because of me? It can't be.

I liked Iris, but this was a summer fling and could be nothing more. She was young, with little experience in relationships. She was going back to Israel and the army.

No, no, she will soon forget about me and this summer romance of hers.

* * *

When Iris returned, I met her at the Karsais' town house for lunch. Lillie and Karel were away at work.

"I'd ask you how you liked California, but you weren't there long enough to find out," I said sarcastically.

"You no understand what happened, it was terrible. I so scared. The guy I go with try to rape me. I have to get plane by myself and leave."

I took a deep breath and exhaled hard. I reached out to her hand. "That's terrible. Are you okay?"

Her eyes glistened with tears. "I'm all right now, but it scary."

"I hate to say I told you so, but this was a bad idea," I said, putting my arm around her.

The tears started to run down her cheeks. "I thought it be okay. I never thought this happen. People in Israel not like this. I don't know why this happen."

"Iris, maybe you don't think so, but you are attractive, and men are men."

Regaining her composure, she wiped away her tears. "I did get to see Hollywood, so it not complete bad," she said with a smile. "Please, no tell Lillie about this, she tell my mother about it and they all get worried. I'm all right now, so it over."

I was amazed at how brave and stoic Iris was about a terrible experience, alone, in a foreign country. I took her face in my hands and gently kissed her on the forehead.

"Aren't you going to ask me if I glad to be back?" she said.

"I guess Monticello, bad as it is, is still better than being raped," I said as I stood up to leave.

"You go to work now before I really angry," she teased as she softly hit me in the stomach. We kissed once, then twice, and I left for work.

* * *

The next several weeks passed quickly. Iris and I would meet for lunch and, when my wallet could afford it, for dinner. Our discussions would often include talking about family.

"My mother so great. She gives me good advice, we like sisters, "Iris said, beaming.

"My mother is a schoolteacher. She's got a good heart but is a little nuts," I said as I stuck my fork into the fried rice.

"Why you say that about your mother?"

"Well, you'd think that, as a schoolteacher, education would be most important to her. My mom had to clean the house. Clean at all hours. Even when I needed my sleep because I had an important exam the next day, she would barge into my room at two a.m., with a vacuum cleaner, no less. Did you ever try to sleep with a vacuum cleaner in your ear?"

"Why you not tell her to wait?" Iris said.

"Because it wouldn't do any good. My mother had her schedule, and if to her it was time to clean the house at two a.m., that's when she would do it. You couldn't change her schedule. She also liked to listen to baseball games. Even the ones that started at eleven at night. She would put the radio on so she could hear it from any room in the house. The games could go on till two or three in the morning. How the hell can you sleep?"

"I think you're mean to your mother," Iris said as she put down her fork and took hold of my wrist.

I looked at her and she returned my gaze. We spent a few seconds looking at each other before she leaned in and planted a kiss on my lips. Her lips were so soft, like melting butter. It wasn't what we said that seemed so important, it was the way she would look at me, question me, always interested in what I had to say. I put my arm around her, pulled her toward me and returned the kiss.

"If we don't stop kissing here, the food will get cold," I said as I released my hold on her and picked up my fork again.

"You the most unromantic person I ever meet," she said, returning her attention back to her plate.

Maybe I was, but there was something about this woman that I wanted more of. Sympathy? Advice? Sex? I didn't know. I just knew I wanted to spend more time with her.

* * *

I didn't think it was getting serious until one evening while driving Iris home from dinner.

"Why you not tell me you date other girls?" Iris asked. Although I was watching the road ahead, I could feel her breath upon my neck as she sat, snuggled against me.

I was taken by surprise. "Who told you that? I don't have a girlfriend now, but I have gone out with other women in the past."

Iris continued to pour hot air onto my neck. "Lillie tell me. It not fair that you go with other girls and me at the same time."

I took a deep breath to give me an extra second to compose myself and turned momentarily to glance at Iris, whose eyes had started to tear.

"Lillie is wrong, I just told you I don't have a steady girlfriend currently, but you don't have the right to tell me who to see. You may be taking this too seriously. I probably will date other women in the future," I said, turning my eyes back to the road to avoid seeing the hurt I was causing her.

I could hear her swallow as the words crept out haltingly. "It not fair you lie to me." Her voice became less tentative but soft and soothing as she took a tissue from her purse to dry her tears. "I felt you cared about me, maybe there something serious between us."

I pulled the car over to the curb and stopped as we reached Lillie's townhouse. Iris's eyes stared directly into mine, seeking an answer while a thin beam of moonlight made her blond hair shine. My hand reached up to cradle my head, and I paused to contemplate how selfish and misleading I had been. I had taken advantage of this woman for my own pleasure, and it was time for me to clarify our relationship.

"Iris, I do like you very much, but we have only been together some six weeks. You are only eighteen and going back to Israel. I am in the middle of taking important exams and trying to decide where to practice. When you go back home you will forget about me." I gave her a minute to mull over what I had said and then gently reached for her hand. "Besides, how do you know how serious you are with me? You said you had only been serious with one other person, and that was for only two weeks."

Iris pulled her hand back and moved closer to the door. I could visualize my words as daggers thrust upon her, each sentence causing more pain. She continued to dry her eyes. Then suddenly she tossed her hair away from her face and said in a loud, firm voice: "No, I sure I want you."

I was speechless. I hadn't the slightest idea why she thought this of me. It just could not be real.

This is just a young girl infatuated with an American who takes her to New York City and out to dinner.

But I had hurt her enough and wanted to let her down easily. I would stall for time. I moved closer to her, took her hand, and said calmly and softly: "Look, I don't know what the future will hold. When you go back home, we can keep in touch. If there really is anything between us, then it should grow. But you need time to see if I'm the one you really want. In the army you will have the opportunity to meet a lot of men and compare them to me."

In an instant Iris fired back. "I've made my choice. I no change my mind. When you come to Israel?"

I rubbed my forehead slowly and looked down as I spoke. "I would love to come to Israel but really haven't given it much thought. I have my exams to finish and then I don't know where I'm going."

Iris bowed her head. "Then you don't want to see me again," she cajoled as the tears returned to her eyes.

I reached out and tried to hold her in my arms. She looked away, opened the car door, and slid out. Wordlessly, she hurried into the house.

Iris had only a couple more weeks before her return to Israel. I didn't want our relationship to end like this.

CHAPTER NINE
Dinner and Discussion

Ten days before Iris was to return to Israel, Lillie, Karel, Steve, Nancy, and I took her out for a goodbye celebration. The restaurant, in a house dating back to the American Revolution, was tucked in a valley of the Catskill mountains. The old stone structure had a very pleasant, relaxed atmosphere. Sitting inside the four-foot-thick rock walls by candlelight, you could peer through the small windows and think you were back in the eighteenth century.

The evening started on a jovial note as I teased Iris that she would not understand the selections on the menu. Iris, by now used to my sarcasm, smiled and lightly punched my arm as she replied: "if you come to Israel. I give you the menu in Hebrew and then I laugh at you."

Despite our flirtatiousness, the conversation became heated as Karel dove into a political discourse over Israel's attack on a terrorist base in Lebanon. "I don't see why Israel puts up with those terrorists. The Israelis should just go in there and wipe them all out. Simple. You just do it once and they learn forever."

Steven jumped in. "Not so simple, Karel. The Arabs have lots of men. If you kill a few, more will take their place. What they need is a permanent solution."

Karel was adamant. "There will never be a solution if there are Arabs. They have wanted Israel destroyed since it was created. Only by fighting can Israel attain its goals. I don't understand these young people, why they want to give captured land back to the Arabs, why they don't fight. Fighting is the way to peace. But young people, like Iris, don't want to fight. They've lost their enthusiasm, their spirit." He raised his voice, put his arm out and pointed a finger toward Iris. "They forget that Jews have obtained everything through strength, and that when we laid our arms down, we were slaughtered. The young people of Israel will learn about strength. They may learn it the hard way, but they will learn."

Iris's face reddened. "Karel, you no live in Israel. It time to give peace a chance. I no want to spend life fighting all the time. I no want to go to the army. I rather go to school. It easy for you to watch TV and then say how we should go fight, while you sit. If you like to fight so much, go to Israel and fight." Her face became taut, teeth clenched, her body stiff like a tiger ready to pounce.

"You don't understand," Karel said raising his voice. "You simply don't know."

Thankfully, Lillie interrupted. "Enough, Karel, Iris is here to enjoy herself, so let's talk about something else."

Nancy changed the topic by asking Iris if she was glad to be returning home. Iris brushed back her hair, which seemed to constantly fall into her face and smiled broadly. Calming down from the earlier conversation she answered: "Yes, I glad. I miss my family very much. I can't wait to see Noah. She must be so big I no recognize her. If not for army I even be happier to go back."

Steven joined the conversation loudly proclaiming, "Oh, you'll like the army. All those men, it will be like a paradise for a young girl. Why if Nancy wasn't married to me, I'm sure she'd volunteer to go with you." He turned toward Nancy and, smiling, rubbed her on the back. "But she was fortunate enough to marry a handsome, rich American doctor."

I knew Steven was kidding, but no one else was laughing. Steven and Nancy kissed as the rest of the table was silent. Turning again to Iris, he said, "I guess you will find a nice pilot and get married."

Iris's smile left her face; she just shrugged, but Steven was not finished. "Iris don't worry. If things really get bad, I will send Bob there to rescue you. They'll figure that if you know such a clod, you're a liability to the country, I can't say as I would blame them. But don't worry: if I could survive the army, you will too."

Iris sat still and erect. Her eyes were open wide, glazed over and expressionless. "There are many things in America that I like—"

"Yes, it's going to be tough to leave all this behind," said Steven, "the big cars, the fancy dinners, all this wealth, to go back and join the army. I'm surprised you haven't thought about staying here. I guess the difference between Americans and Israelis is that Israelis have a cause and a conscience. If it was me, I'd stay here. But then again that means staying here with *Bob*, so maybe I'd go." Steven chuckled.

I was used to Steven's ribbing and gave a half smile as the rest of the table sat silently looking around for the waiter, trying to ignore what they had just heard. Iris looked down at her lap, her hair flopping over her face.

Steven saw her discomfort. "Iris, what is wrong? You're so quiet. Don't be so sad. At least you're leaving Monticello."

Karel added. "Steven is right—we should be sad we're staying here."

Lillie had more knowledge than Karel or Steven of Iris's feelings toward me. "Now stop it. Monticello is not so bad. Besides, it is only natural that Iris be a little sad. She had an exceptionally good time here."

Iris took hold of my hand under the table and rested it on her lap as Lillie continued: "Yes, I think Iris had a very good time here. She saw New York City, a Broadway play, California, and met a young doctor. I'd say not bad for a few weeks."

Now, squeezing my hand, Iris raised her head, smiled, and looked at me. "Israel better, but America not all bad."

The waiter arrived with our dinner, temporarily halting the discussion.

Later, as dinner was winding down to dessert, Steven again dominated the conversation. "Iris, do you think you will ever come back to the US?"

Iris hesitated as she placed her hand to her forehead. "I do not know. I have two years in army; after that I not know—"

Steven did not let her finish, waving his arms in the air. "Now that you've tasted the good life, I bet you'll be back."

Iris did not respond. She looked at me with a blank expression as if nothing she said to Steven would have any effect, then turned away.

With dinner finished, we headed back to the cars. Iris wanted me to take her home instead of riding with Karel and Lillie. As soon as she slid into the passenger seat, she turned toward me to say what she thought of Steven.

"He no let me speak, he always interrupt me. He think he always right and want to be center of attention."

"Steven doesn't mean everything he says, you have to know where his heart lies," I said.

She loudly and slowly responded: "I no care where his heart be. He make me feel like a fool. He know that I not know English very well. Why he not let me speak? I no like him. I'm sorry."

She turned away from me and looked straight ahead at the road. The topic was closed as we drove back to Monticello. It was obvious that Steven and Iris didn't get along. It was also obvious Iris had strong opinions. She was not to be intimidated by Karel or Steven—maybe nobody. I felt this woman's youth belied her inner strength. These were qualities I much admired.

But in ten days our relationship would end.

CHAPTER TEN
Time to Return

*I*t was the beginning of September and a few days before Iris's return to Israel. I wanted to give her a parting gift. Iris had been more than a casual friend. I wanted her to fondly remember this time, even if it was now ending. Deciding on a gold locket I had the phrase "To a Special Person" inscribed on the back. Iris was special. She had street wisdom above her age. It took her fifteen minutes to discern the malevolence between me and my brother. I was still in a quagmire over it after thirty years. She was a good listener. If I was sarcastic, she could give it right back. And add to this a good sense of humor and great looks. What was there not to like?

But I reiterated to myself that this was not a lasting relationship. She was young and inexperienced. She would go back to Israel and date other men and soon forget me.

Two days before Iris was to leave, I picked up the locket and went over to Lillie's to say goodbye. Iris opened the door and went into the living room as I followed. I crept up behind her and told her not to move as I slipped the locket around her neck. Iris took the locket in her hand, staring at it as she turned it over in her palm. A big smile lit her face as I read the inscription to her. She threw her hands around me and whispered in my ear, "I love you." She held me fast, kissing me on the lips and holding me so tight I thought I was going to lose consciousness. I had only met Iris a few weeks earlier. I hardly knew her and didn't want to profess a false love. I felt guilty for being unable to return her feelings for me and didn't know what to say.

Iris finally released her hold on me and again looked down at the locket. "I think it very beautiful; I will never take it off." She then again grabbed me in an embrace and planted several kisses on my lips. Pulling back a few inches from me she asked, "You come to Israel? When?"

Iris had repeatedly asked this question and I always tried to be noncommittal. I didn't want to have to face her disappointment by saying no and didn't want to make a promise I had no intention of fulfilling. "I'll try to come, maybe in April. That's about eight months away, but I don't know. I 'll just try my best."

Iris moved back farther from me. As she looked into my eyes I could see the glint of tears forming. "You come; I hope you come. I want to see you so much, but I fear you never get there. Maybe you just tell me this, so I stop asking you."

Is she reading my mind?

"No, no, that's not true," I said, even though I knew it was, my voice rising in defense. "I just don't want to make any promises I can't keep. So many things can happen between now and April." I tried to change the tone of the conversation by jokingly adding, "You may meet a general and fall in love and not want to see me again."

Iris's blush highlighted her freckles; her back and shoulders stiffened; she took in a gulp of air and exhaled. "You think you're so funny. I no want general. I want you and I will miss you very much. Maybe I die waiting till April to see you, but I know I want you."

I stopped smiling as I continued to look directly at her. "Give yourself a chance before you profess such love. Take the time to grow up some. You're only eighteen."

Iris was beginning to cry. "I not need time to grow up, I know my mind. I love you but you no love me. If you not want to again say it, it will be better than lying to me."

Her love, I was sure, would die a natural death, but I wanted her to be the one to realize it. I didn't want to hurt her. "I'm not lying to you I do want to see you again, but I can't predict the future and I don't want to say I'm in love with you when I'm not. Let time decide whether there is love between us," I said as she reached for a tissue from the side table.

She wiped tears from her eyes. "I'll be right back; I got something for you."

She went upstairs and returned with a box and presented it to me. Inside was a wallet. Looking at it I lost my voice and started to tear. With so little money and so many people back home to bring presents to she had used some of her funds to buy this gift. Something inside of me made me want more of this woman, this woman I thought I could never have. Maybe, just maybe I could fool the both of us into thinking we would meet again.

"You make my life so complicated. I promise you I'll write and call and do all I can to visit you in April," I said as I reached to hold her and kiss her lips. We stopped talking as we held each other for a few minutes. I wished her a safe trip back home and good luck in the army; she wished me the same in my exams. Then we kissed again, and I left.

When I returned to Steven and Nancy's home, I looked at the wallet. Inside there was a card in carefully written English block letters: "Somethings never change with time, my love for you. I miss you. Iris Klein."

CHAPTER ELEVEN
Communicating from Israel

I was confident that Iris and I would go our separate ways. However, a few days after her return to Israel, my secretary, Rose, came in with a message from the wire service. The short note read: "Call me immediately, very important, Iris."

I raced home and called, expecting some terrible news. *Is she hurt? Did something happen to her family?*

"Iris, is that you? "I said.

It was hard to hear clearly through the phone static as she answered. "Hello, Bob, hello." It sounded like someone talking at a loud disco with their mouth full.

"Are you okay? I got your message today. What's wrong? It sounded urgent," I said.

"I miss you. I miss you very much."

"But what's wrong? Why the urgency?"

Iris raised her voice. "That is what is wrong."

I started to raise my voice in anger. "You mean you send me a message that makes me think something terrible has happened just to tell me you miss me? I thought some tragedy had occurred. Why didn't you write that you miss me? it's a lot cheaper."

Iris's tone softened. "Why you so mad? That very important to me. I just want to talk to you."

My anger melted as I felt humbled that she still thought so much of me. "Well, I'm glad you did. I'm happy to hear your voice."

We discussed her family and how glad she was to see them, but really, the conversation was of little note. When the call was over, I was ecstatic but didn't know why.

Is it because I have deeper feelings for her than I realized?

That evening I penned my first letter to her. I told her about work, the weather, Steven and Nancy, and concluded with what I felt was most important.

I hope you write to me about your feelings, because communication will be so very important to us, especially as we are so many miles apart. Now you will find out whether you really want me or whether it was a passing fancy of the summer.

Until we are in touch again, my warmest regards,
Bob

I was still certain that with time she would find someone else. *Am I hoping that someone else is me?*

* * *

Studying dragged on as I sought to prove that if I memorized enough irrelevant junk, it would mean I understood the important information as well. I still had not received any decent job offers and instead decided on another year of advanced training in ophthalmic surgery by applying for a paid fellowship. I was doing little surgery in Monticello and there were new procedures that I wanted to learn. Another year of study would not be a waste of time and it would give me an additional opportunity to find a permanent job opening. I still hoped that Steven and I would work together, but it was obvious Monticello was not the place. He was a good ophthalmologist, honest and inquisitive. We both wanted to give the most advanced care to our patients. Surely, as brothers, we could work out our differences. I hoped that he would change and become more amenable to some business compromise we could both live with.

A few days after my phone call to Iris I received a letter from her.

Two years in army it's a long time and I don't know what will haped in that time. I hope that you will come but as you tolled me, I don't think that you entendted to come at all so what I had to do is to wait and see what hapend? I hope that everything will be as I want. In the first month in the army that month we trend all the time and I don't know if I can write to you so if you want to here from me (I don't think so) you can call me person to person in Saturday and if I'll be home, I'll be glad to here from you.

Miss and love,
Iris

In deciding on a place to go for the next year, I wrote inquiring about an opening in Texas. I knew nothing about Texas. The practice was in a town I couldn't even find on a map. However, this practice was owned by a famous ophthalmologist in advanced surgical techniques. He was performing over forty cataract operations a week. He lectured all over the United States and internationally. I didn't think I'd end up there, but it appeased my mind to at least apply. Texas seemed way too far from New York, and I was hoping for an equally good opportunity closer.

Each week I penned a letter to Iris. I didn't want to admit to myself that maybe I did have feelings for her, that I didn't want our relationship to end. Usually, the letter was a rehash of the one from the previous week.

Dear Iris,

It is hard for me to make definite promises as I haven't made up my own mind about what to do. I still want to see you in Israel this spring, but what will happen between now and then I don't know. I hope that you don't forget me, but I also want you to see other men to decide for yourself whether I'm the one you really want.

Bob

The fellowship in Texas accepted me. They required a decision by December. As I had nothing else, I accepted. Iris and I talked on the phone once a week. The connection was usually so poor that every word had to be repeated twice. Of course, paying by the minute was like paying the full price for half the message. By the time we said hello, how are you, how is your family, the time that I could afford had elapsed. Anything of substance was hard to discuss while I watched the minutes, and the dollars wash away.

One morning Steven dashed into my room at 4:30 a.m. and, shaking me vigorously, awakened me. "Bob, get out of bed, it's Iris on the phone. Would you please tell your girlfriend not to call at this hour? We have to go to work, and I can't work when I've been up the whole night answering your phone," he said loudly, turned, and stormed out. As there was no phone in my room, I ran down the hall to the kitchen to speak. As in the past I was worried that something terrible must have happened for her to call at this time. And again, I was wrong. We tried to communicate, repeating each sentence several times until enough words came through the static that we could understand. I tried to tell her about the time difference. Israel was seven hours ahead of eastern standard time. I was sure she must know but didn't care, as she felt it imperative to talk to me.

"I in army now. It terrible. I hate it," she said.

This was nothing new. I inquired what could be so bad.

"It all secret. I just very tired and want you to come. I no can wait so long. You come!" she demanded.

As with all the past similar requests, all I could say was that I would try to come but we should write more to express our feelings. I tried to tell her how expensive these calls were. It was about a hundred dollars for thirty minutes.

"Everything with you money. I need to talk to you. I so unhappy in army and I need to have you," Iris said angrily.

Flying to Israel to rescue Iris from the army was not a reason to travel. When I told her this, there was just silence on the other end. It seemed so long a pause that I asked her if she was okay.

Softly she responded yes. Then a pause followed by "Bob, I love you." She then hung up.

I went back to bed and awakened some hours later not sure of what had transpired. I felt uncomfortable. Life was too complicated to be communicated over the phone. I sat down to write a letter to try to sum up our relationship and the potential future.

Dear Iris,

Think a second for yourself about what your life would be like if you married me. You might have to go to Texas with me. You may not realize your dream to continue your education as your life would be tied to my career. When we move it might not be to a place with a college for you to study. At eighteen, are you willing to give up your dreams and hopes to marry? I don't doubt your maturity for your age but what I fear is your missing the parts of life that age has not let you experience. That is why I want you to go out in Israel and enjoy yourself. Love doesn't tarnish with age or comparison, if two people are really meant for each other.

Bob

I felt she was overdoing our relationship. Marriage was not in my mind. I wanted her to stop dreaming and be more realistic. Repeatedly I told myself she would make new friendships, find new lovers. That with time she would realize that this was an infatuation that she had matured from. I cared for her, but I just could not see any future, given that we lived so far apart. She too would see the futility of continuing and move on. It would be less hurtful, to her, for me not to break off our relationship but to let her decide when that time had arrived, as I was still sure it would. I would be sorry when that time came, but at thirty-one, I could handle the breakup better than she could.

CHAPTER TWELVE
The Exam

I passed the written part of my exams in October and was getting ready for the oral exam, to be held in May in Philadelphia. Life in Monticello was becoming more amicable. I started paying the rent on time and Steven dropped his demand for compensation for the very few surgical patients I operated on. My social life even included a few dates, but nothing serious. The memory of Iris lingered in my mind in comparison to whoever I went out with. Although I had told Iris that I would try to visit Israel in April, now I had good reason to decline. I wanted nothing to interfere with my preparation for the oral exam.

Between October and April, Iris and I communicated by mail and phone. There was nothing new in the correspondence. She hated the army and begged me to come visit her, and I kept telling her to go out with other men. But with each month, her tenacity for hanging on to our relationship increasingly instilled a feeling on my part that this was more than a momentary infatuation.

She really wants me.

It was no longer proper for me to lead her on, waiting for her to forget me. I had to decide if I loved this woman or not. But as May and my oral exams were approaching, I put off any decision about Iris.

On the bus to Philadelphia, I kept thinking of possible questions I'd be asked. Whenever I thought of a question I couldn't answer, beads of sweat would appear. I brought a textbook with me to find the answers and alleviate this panic.

All the candidates stayed at the same hotel, which was also where the test was held. We tried to give each other confidence and, most of all, fortify our own confidence as we inquired, subtly, what each other knew.

"Hey, Bob, good to see you. How you been?" a fellow resident called out.

"Pretty good, John. How about you?"

"Fine, I'll be a lot better after this test," he said in a low, almost prayer-like response.

I too was anxious and at this point just wanted to get it over with. "I wish it would start; this waiting is terrible. And we have three days of this garbage. If you foul up the first session, do they send you home early?" It was not common knowledge how the test was administered, although many rumors were circulating. Maybe John knew more.

"No, they let you take the whole thing. There are seven parts. You can flunk two and must repeat those sessions. But flunk three and you get to take the whole thing over again. You're not nervous?" John asked, smiling.

I drew in a deep breath and hoped my voice wouldn't crack in betrayal. "Well, I'd rather be doing something else. I only hope I studied enough." I wondered how anyone could have studied more.

"Got to go. See you later. Good luck," John said as he turned to leave.

I went back to my room because I couldn't stand to see all the applicants asking each other questions that I might not know. I called my brother for a shoulder to cry on. He reiterated that no mortal could have studied more than I had. That should have made me feel better, but I kept on thinking that if I failed, after all I had done to prepare, I would never be able to pass.

In the morning, the first part of the orals started innocently enough. I waited outside one of the examining rooms for my turn to enter. As I sat, telling myself how bright I was, one of the examiners rushed out of the room.

"Where is Dr. Blum?" he asked the secretary guarding us.

She looked around the waiting area. "I don't see him, but I'll find him."

The examiner frowned. "Tell him that I have a borderline candidate that I want him to make the final decision on."

All my confidence crumbled as I realized they were playing this game for real. The poor candidate soon exited the room, head down in defeat. As I watched him disappear in the fluorescent lights, I heard my name called.

Are they crazy? They want me to go into the same room where they have just slain this innocent student?

I half expected to see a room covered in blood. However, smiling faces greeted me. The examiners introduced themselves and shook my trembling, sweaty hand. They had two sets of books but only one with answers. Naturally, they didn't mix the books up.

"Dr. Jaffee, on page seven, can you identify the pathology?" the first inquisitor began.

"I believe it is epithelial downgrowth," I stuttered out.

Is that correct? Why doesn't he say yes or no?

The examiner was so stone-faced, he should've worked for the CIA. "If it is as you say Dr. Jaffee, what other things would you look for on examination?"

I ran off four or five responses, but the examiner was still hungry. "What else would you do, Dr. Jaffee, what else?"

My mind investigated all its cubby holes but alas there was nothing more to be found. In a soft voice, I answered dejectedly: "I don't believe I would do anything else."

It was obvious from his expression that we weren't members of the same faith. He proceeded. "Turn to page sixty-one. What is that?"

I looked at it for some time, but I could not identify it.

The examiner impatiently asked, "Well, Doctor, what do you think?"

I could feel the sweat form on my forehead. "I'm not sure."

The examiner started to tap the desk with his fingers. "Could it be herpes or sarcoid or tuberculosis?"

"It could be a million things. I'm just not sure which one it is," I blurted out in panic. When the instructor went out to call in Dr. Blum, I imagined I was soon to follow the previous student into the sunset of the fluorescent lights.

Dr. Blum took his seat behind the desk, grabbed the exam book and looked up at me without expression. "I've just got a few simple questions to ask you."

This was my last chance. I was not sure of the answer to the question he asked. I repeated my answer twice. Each time Dr. Blum asked me if I wanted to change my response.

I stuck to my answer; I had to sound confident if I wanted to pass this section.

Dr. Blum, also stone-faced, replied. "Okay, you can go."

I got up, relieved I was finished. "Did I pass?" I asked in a high-pitched squeal.

Dr. Blum rose from the desk. "You'll find out. Good day," he said curtly, pointing to the door.

My head bent, my legs shaking, I walked out of the room. I thought there was no use continuing as I probably flunked the first part out of seven. But for the next two days I went in and out of rooms.

The final session ended with the examiner asking me if I knew of a drug to prevent some viral infection. Again, the cupboards upstairs in my mind were bare. He smiled. He said he didn't know of any either but wanted to see if I knew something he didn't. Fortunately, for his life and my jail sentence, he shook my hand and told me how well I knew my material.

I returned to Monticello thinking I had not passed the entire exam. To my surprise, a few days later, congratulations on my successful completion came in the mail. This was the culmination of college, medical school, internship, and residency. I was now a board-certified ophthalmologist. But with only a few days until I left for Texas, there was no time to celebrate.

I packed and soon was loading up the car.

I looked at Monticello one more time. The mountains and trees were as beautiful as the economy and town were pathetic.

Standing in the driveway of Steven's house II said my goodbyes to Lillie, Karel, Steven, and Nancy. They hugged me and wished me the best.

"Bob, remember we love you." Steven's parting words.

It was the end of May 1980. I was off to Odessa, Texas, wherever that was.

CHAPTER THIRTEEN
Odessa, Texas

O dessa, Texas, was unlike any place I had seen. It was a land of too little or too much. Too little water, trees, and natural beauty, too much sand and heat. It had once been a sea, the Permian Basin, but all that was left was endless beach. It was so flat that Columbus would have thought himself mistaken when he judged the world to be round. Dotted haphazardly were numerous pumping oil derricks that from afar looked like giant praying mantises in a horror movie. That people lived there surely proved that God had a sense of humor.

My first stop in Odessa was my new place of employment, Sheets Associated. This was truly an impressive operation. Physically, it was huge, a warehouse for the practice of ophthalmology. The building, once a storage facility, had been converted to a health clinic. The inside was a maze of little rooms connected by meandering hallways. I had trained at New York University but the facilities here were more impressive. There were nurses, insurance workers, secretaries, computer operators, ophthalmic technicians, all dedicated to ophthalmology. Covering everything was the mass of patients who came from all over Texas and New Mexico as well as from the eastern states like Massachusetts to see Dr. Sheets. He was world famous for his innovative surgery.

Upon my arrival I was ushered into his office. The office was big enough to be a movie theater. In the rear was a large wooden desk with ornate carving. A big, plush, executive type of leather chair was behind it. The open area in front of the desk seemed large enough for a football game. The floor was covered by a deep red carpet, and the front wall had a screen that retracted into the ceiling.

I sat for a few minutes, waiting for Dr. Sheets. Through the door came a sixtyish, portly man. He wore enough gold jewelry that when the light shone on him, he looked like the burning bush from the ten commandments. I stood up to shake his hand.

"Good morning, Dr. Jaffee. I hope you had a pleasant trip. Is there anything you need to get settled?" Dr. Sheets said in a deep, friendly voice, smiling.

As I didn't have any place to stay and was using a motel room temporarily, I asked for his assistance. He was gracious in offering his driver and limo to take me to see various apartments, as I didn't know the area.

"When can you start work?"

I squinted as light reflected off his huge gold belt buckle. "In a couple of days. I just need to find a place to stay and take care of some personal things, and I'll be ready."

Dr. Sheets smiled again, obviously pleased at my eagerness. He got up, summoned his driver, Roger, for me and disappeared into the mass of waiting assistants and patients.

A few minutes later the driver arrived, and we were off in the limousine. Roger was Dr. Sheet's "man Friday." He drove for Dr. Sheets, gathered his slides for medical presentations, packed his luggage, picked up his laundry. In short, Roger did whatever Dr. Sheets requested.

It was May, but the temperature was already in the nineties, and it was dry—very dry. Roger drove showing me the sights of Odessa. The buildings were mostly one or two stories with an occasional multi storied building. The hospital seemed modern as was the high school, Permian High with "Mojo" written on the façade. What mojo was I had no idea sounded like some voodoo thing to me. We stopped at various apartment complexes until I found a vacancy close to the clinic.

It all seemed like a dream. A few days earlier, I had been in a one-room office with Rose, my combination nurse, bill collector, and secretary. Now I was in a chauffeured limo and working in a place where I had to ask directions to get to the front door.

It didn't take long to get settled, however, and I was soon ready to start work.

The surgical volume as well as the variety of medical cases was enormous. Work proceeded smoothly, with a chance to see and practice what I had learned in my training besides gaining new knowledge and surgical skills. The personnel in the clinic were a new breed to me. They were very helpful, even if I couldn't understand their Texas drawl. However, I got even as they didn't understand my speed or pronunciation, being from New York, either. For the first few weeks we repeated many of our sentences.

To get a better perspective on the town and meet some of the local women, I went out to one of the dance halls. I wore my going-out clothes—dress slacks and shirt, with penny loafers—as I usually did in New York.

The hall was dark, with a haphazard collection of wooden tables and chairs that looked like they had been rescued after someone tried to destroy them. Onstage was a band flanked by a Confederate flag and the flag of Texas. I guess they hadn't come to terms with being part of the United States. The floor was covered with sawdust and peanut shells, the latter from barrels of peanuts in the room.

In the darkness I could make out forms like moving mushrooms, six feet tall. These turned out to be humans with cowboy hats. No one, save me, wore anything but blue jeans and cowboy boots. Even the dancing was alien to me. Men pushing their women in front of them in a continuous circle. I later learned that this was the Texas two-step.

Finding an empty table, I dropped into a chair and put my feet up on the table as the other patrons were doing. My black penny loafers were like a lighthouse beacon among the ubiquitous cowboy boots. When the waitress came over, I didn't want to speak as my accent made me fear I could be captured. Luckily, she said, "Beer?" and I just nodded yes. Every now and then, one of the patrons would feel the need for self-expression by jumping on a table, waving his hat, and yelling, "Whoopee!" Occasionally the women, believing in equal rights, would join in.

Even the songs had a very unsettling quality. I had never heard "Up Against the Wall Redneck Mother." Overall, a most "elegant" place.

It was obvious that for me to tackle Texas, the first thing was not to look and act like I came from New York.

As it didn't seem that I was going to meet anyone at the local bars, my main connection to Texas was through my work. My first friend was Charles, an internist. He worked at the hospital doing the preop physical exams. He invited me over for dinner and I was happy to accept.

"Bob, it's good to see one of you Yankees we can tolerate," Charles said as he spit some tobacco juice into a cup. He introduced me to his wife, Mary, and we were soon engaged in conversation as we ate. I repeated to them my adventures into Texas society and my difficulty meeting people.

"Oh, you poor thing," Mary said sympathetically.

"Now Bob, you can't let those women get the better of you. You got to just go up to them and treat them like dirt," Charles said in his slow Texas drawl. "You're probably use to treating women too nicely, and they just don't respect a man down here who treats them well. Why, I used to sit at home when I treated the women like ladies, but I learned, Bob, and you will too." His smile widened as he realized, to himself, the truth of his statement.

"Oh, that's not true," Mary added in protest, her voice sweet and cajoling.

Charles replied emphasizing every word. "Yes, it is. Women feel that a man who treats them well isn't worth much. They respect a man who can treat them like garbage, it makes them work harder to be accepted." Charles put his hand on my shoulder. "Now I don't want to hear about you going to those clubs and sitting in the corner. You go up to one of them pretty ones, pinch her on the ass and ask her out."

I was certainly getting an education in Texas culture. This was not my idea of how to treat a woman. I saw myself more likely to end up pinned to the wall of a bar as a Yankee war trophy before I could adapt to this lifestyle.

Dinner was followed by watching the news on TV. One of the stories concerned Israel. This gave me the opportunity to tell Charles and Mary about Iris in Israel. I told them I was worried about her safety in the army. Charles turned toward me on the sofa and again in his deliberate, slow, authoritative tone gave his prediction.

"Now Bob, you needn't worry, because God watches over those people. It says so in the bible: those are God's chosen people."

"They may be chosen but they can still get killed," I said.

Charles said without hesitation, "You should read the bible. It tells about Israel; it tells of all that has come and prophesizes what will come to pass. It tells about the invaders coming to Israel and how Israel will throw them back."

I was not much of a bible thumber. "Maybe you're right. We'll let time be the judge. I must be up early tomorrow. It's been delightful. Thank you for dinner," I said, getting up to leave.

Charles had the last word. "I know I'm right. It's all in the book, all there for us to know."

So, these were some of the people of Texas. I had heard about people who took the bible literally but never met anyone who did so until I met Charles. On the way back to my apartment I laughed to myself. I was not sure which culture was more foreign to me—Texas or Israel.

CHAPTER FOURTEEN
New Friends

One of the dreaded duties of physicians is being on call. You are attached to an electronic pager with a mind of its own dedicated to interrupting you at the most inconvenient times. One night while sitting at home watching TV, the pager decided that I was too comfortable and went off. I answered the call and was soon on my way to the office to deal with the emergency. Two young women arrived, one with a towel over her eyes, who I assumed was the patient.

"What happened?" I said to the patient's companion.

An attractive woman who looked to be about thirty identified herself as Diane. "Now you won't believe this. My husband and I were celebrating our third wedding anniversary when Bertha, our waitress, opened a bottle of champagne and the cork flew off into her eye. Now have you ever heard of anything so stupid?"

As I was writing this all down in the allotted space on the chart for "history," I had to admit this was a bit unusual.

I sat Bertha behind the slit-lamp (an instrument that magnifies and illuminates the eye) and took the towel from her face. Bertha had a *hyphema*, which is a bleed in the front of the eye, what is called the anterior chamber of the eye. I examined her taking her visual acuity and the pressure in her eye. The acuity was down due to the blood obscuring her vision. Her intraocular pressure was normal. The blood would reabsorb, and she would be fine if no further damage resulted and the bleeding did not reoccur. I told her to stay home on strict bed rest and gave her a return appointment for the next day.

"Look, I'm really sorry for ruining your evening," Diane said as she helped Bertha up from the examining chair. "Why don't you join me and my husband and help us celebrate? We'd be glad to have you."

I was surprised at the offer. I never had a patient invite me to dinner for taking care of them, especially people I had never met. I tried to joke. "I don't know, are you sure it's safe?"

Diane chuckled. "I guess as long as you don't have any champagne, you should be okay."

I thought about it for a second and decided to go as I had nothing else planned and wanted to socialize more in Odessa. "Okay, where are you located?"

"Meet us at Pelican's, on Fifth Street. I'll take Bertha home and meet you there. My husband is at the restaurant now, so you can go and ask for Curtis Johnson. You can't miss him. Just look for a man alone at a table with a bucket of champagne."

I still thought it a strange way to meet people, but what the hell.

* * *

It was night and very quiet as I parked my car at the restaurant. A light breeze was welcome in the July heat. I entered Pelican's, a steak house, through the stained glass decorated front door. Families, couples young and old sat behind plates of ribeye. It was crowded and noisy. Voices mixed with the sound of glasses finding their mark on the table and cutlery scratching the bottom of plates. I passed the hostess telling her I was joining another group. Looking around the room I spotted a middle-aged man, alone, puffing on a cigarette with a champagne bucket by his side. I weaved my way around the closely placed tables and approached. "Curtis, I presume. My name is Bob Jaffee. I am the ophthalmologist that examined your waitress, and your wife invited me over for a drink. I hope I'm not intruding on your celebration," I said, extending my hand.

"Well, sit-down, brother, and pour yourself a drink," Curtis replied, getting up to shake my hand. He was the image of Texas on two legs: about six foot two and lanky, wearing cowboy boots and a wide leather belt with a rattlesnake buckle. His moustache resembled the horns of a Texas steer, and his voice was deep and intense, his words seeming to gain volume as he spoke. He pulled a chair out for me.

I still felt the situation was awkward. "It's kind of strange, meeting people like this. Again, I hope this is not an intrusion."

Not upset in the least, Curtis replied: "Mercy man, no. Any friend of Diane's is a friend of mine. Grab a glass and I'll pour you some champagne."

Curtis was so sincere, so unassuming, I felt I had known him for years. As he filled my glass, I reverted to my New York manner of asking questions. "What do you do?"

"I'm a hairdresser, been here for seven years. Dr. Jaffee. How about you?"

"Please, call me Bob. No need to be so formal. I came down from New York to work with Dr. Sheets for a year. He uses a lot of innovative surgical techniques that I want to learn."

Curtis refilled his glass. "Well, do you think you'll stay?"

"I don't know. I've only been here a couple of months, so it's kind of soon to tell for me," I said as I toyed with my drink, cognizant of the fact that I was still on call.

We continued to talk, not noticing that Diane had returned.

"I'm so sorry for interrupting your evening, but I was concerned—" she said as she addressed me, pulled out a chair and sat down.

"Now Bob, if it was a dog that had an eye injury, Diane could have taken care of it, but seeing that it was human, we didn't want to take any chances," said Curtis.

Diane blushed. "Oh, Curtis."

"No, really man, Diane here is a veterinarian," Curtis said.

I was surprised at their discrepancy in careers. Diane had the more prestigious career and probably made more money. My biased opinion was that the careers should have been switched. *Well, I might as well toast their relationship even if I don't understand it.*

"How about a toast to your anniversary and to bottles without corks," I said, raising my glass.

"Hey man, I can drink to that," Curtis said as he downed his champagne.

"You can drink to anything," Diane said.

"Glad to have you here, Bob. Have something to eat with us," Curtis said, pouring himself more champagne.

"No thanks. I just ate before the emergency call, but please go ahead," I said waving my hand across the table.

We continued to talk about where I was from and my limited adventures in Texas, to which Curtis exclaimed, "You're beautiful, man, I love it," stamping his feet, laughing, and pouring more champagne.

I felt extremely at ease with Curtis and Diane. We exchanged telephone numbers and talked away the evening. I was sorry the time had passed so quickly, but it was late, and I was still on call. I said my goodbyes and said we would soon meet again.

Yes, there are some fine people in Texas.

CHAPTER FIFTEEN
Planning a Decision

*T*he days passed under the hottest sun I had ever experienced. The temperature was ninety to a hundred degrees for weeks at a time.

Now July, it had been eleven months since Iris left for Israel. We corresponded intermittently by mail and phone. I told her about my work. She complained about the army and taking orders. I kidded her that marriage was like the army, except the orders came from the husband. She was quick to point out that that certainly was not her definition of marriage. She didn't say much about her experience in the army, as it was classified.

The relationship stalled on the same conversation of my coming to Israel, how much she loved me, and her frustration at waiting for me, considering I might never arrive. Iris was a great person, but I didn't think I needed to go to Israel to find a companion. Certainly, in the States, even in alien Texas, I would find a mate.

Surgery was becoming more plentiful. I was soon doing new and more complicated procedures.

Steven and I still planned to work together sometime in the future. I still thought it possible we could work out our financial disputes. My father's favorite, he was the older brother I admired. Growing up, it was instilled in me that Steven 's approval of anything was paramount. He had a hold on me I couldn't shake. If he wanted something, it must be right. And he wanted us to work together. I told him about all the new procedures I was learning. I invited him down to Odessa to watch me operate. He could practice in the animal lab. It would give him a chance to learn new techniques and see me at work. Besides, it was tax deductible.

Having been in Texas for a couple of months, with few people who could understand me when I asked for directions to the men's room much less carry on a conversation, I would welcome his visit. I had also decided to give in and buy my first pair of cowboy boots. I tried on several pairs, but they all hurt my feet. The height of the boot and the tight fit made me feel as if my ankle was fused. No wonder real cowboys rode horses. These things were too uncomfortable to walk in. However, I felt this was something I absolutely needed.

Armed with this new accessory to give me a feeling of security, I again headed to the bars. I was the only one constantly staring down at his feet. It didn't occur to me till I lost sight of them in the darkness that nobody cared about my new boots. As I watched these Texas make-believe cowboys pick up women, I felt that I, with my new boots, could do the same.

An attractive woman was standing alone on the dance floor. *A perfect opportunity.*

I set myself on the target. "Care to dance?"

The girl accepted and we were off. The music picked up, but I didn't. We kept on bumping into people on the dance floor.

"Hey fella, watch where the hell you're going," said an irate mushroom as we grazed him and his girl.

My partner stepped back from me and angrily exclaimed, "You are the clumsiest son of a bitch I ever seen." She was obviously more upset than I was. I guess they took this counterclockwise rotation as no frivolous matter.

Well, my boots and I were going nowhere. I left the bar, got a bottle of liquor, returned home, and drank myself to sleep.

The next morning, after a breakfast of aspirin, I thought of Iris. I could talk to her, laugh with her, complain to her. There was nothing for me in Texas. Every time I tried to engage in Texas culture, I was reminded of how I didn't belong. But I had to know if it was just loneliness or if, despite all the women in the United States, I was falling in love with an Israeli.

I didn't think about our differences in age and culture. I didn't think about the separation of distance or whether I would work in Israel or the United States. I had to find out.

Is this the woman I want as my wife?

Dear Iris,

I have decided to come to Israel in December. I want to find out if we should spend the rest of our lives together. I don't understand why I keep thinking of you —we only knew each other for several weeks —but I feel I must see you either to end our relationship or bind it.

You are correct when you say that you are still a girl with a lot to learn, but learning to cook and care for a house is not the same as learning to care for a spouse. Nor could I give you the emotional strength you would need to handle me or any other man. You must have at this time the maturity to handle feelings of jealousy, loneliness, or boredom; to cope with a husband when he is depressed; to share your feelings; and to demand your own freedom of expression and a life separate from your mate's.

These traits you must have before marriage, for no marriage can survive in a storm if each person is floundering to find his or her own identity. If you have this stability and we find in each other what we desire in a husband or wife, then we need not fear differences in culture, language, or lifestyle.

In the end, only a lack of communication between and within ourselves can defeat a marriage.

Love,
Bob

I mailed the letter, feeling at ease that I was finally going to bring a resolution to our affair. It was 1980, and this was my idea of what a marriage should be. The woman was to take care of the house, children, and the cooking. She was to lend emotional support to her husband. The man brought home the paycheck. It was what I had learned from the TV shows I watched growing up in the fifties and sixties. I remembered the show *Father Knows Best*. There was never any show called *Mother Knows Best*. It was the way my own parents had done it. Even though my mother worked, she cleaned the house and did the cooking. My father paid the bills. It was never a question as to who did what.

* * *

There was little to keep me occupied in Odessa besides my work. Being on call every other day, I didn't have to worry much about free time.

Scheduling got so tight that it was difficult finding time for a haircut. Luckily Curtis had hours as bad as mine and could see me even at nine at night. He cut hair with a beer in one hand and a comment on everything.

"Bob, I think it's beautiful you're here. You know, man, I don't like many people first off, but when I met you, I knew you were a great person," he said as the scissors whizzed passed by ear.

"Curtis, even my mother is still deciding whether I'm a nice guy. How could you be so sure?" I quipped.

Curtis stopped cutting and started waving the comb and scissors like he was conducting an orchestra. "No, really, man. The way you came out to help Diane and Bertha that night, we really appreciate it, we really do."

"Well thanks, but I was just doing my job. Don't make me such a hero."

Curtis went back to cutting my hair. "Well, maybe so, man, but we think it was terrific. Bertha is doing a lot better also."

I told Curtis about Iris and my upcoming visit to Israel. He seemed more enthusiastic than I was.

"I know about those Israelis. They are one industrious people. If you're lucky enough to marry one, you just bring her back here and I will show her around."

I had no idea how Curtis knew anything about Israelis, but he seemed to know something about everything. He was an expert at keeping a conversation going. He never let it drop, always appearing interested. As he poured himself another beer, he told me about the places to see in Texas, about the vegetation and the insects. He would finish one beer then start another as he jumped effortlessly from the sexual differences of one bug versus another.

"Curtis, aren't you afraid that if you keep pushing those beers, you're going to get drunk?" I asked as he opened another can.

Curtis again stopped cutting and just stood in front of me, raising his voice. "Hell no, man. You know, when I was in Vietnam, the doctors couldn't believe the way I metabolize things. My body breaks down things so fast that it's unbelievable. I could drink all day and not feel it. I guess I'm just a medical phenomenon," he said, resuming the haircut.

I thought this a sure sign he was drunk, but his hands seemed calm, and my head was still on my shoulders as he continued to cut away. We decided to go to dinner with Diane later in the week as he finished my hair, his last beer, and a lecture on the sex life of mosquitos in unison.

CHAPTER SIXTEEN
Preparations

I started to plan for my trip to Israel. I didn't know if Iris still wanted to marry me, and I was totally unsure of what I wanted. However, I thought it best to be prepared for any eventuality. I called the US Immigration office in El Paso to find out how I could bring Iris into the States. Immigration Services informed me that I could bring Iris back on a fiancée visa. If I expressed an intention to marry, she could come to the United States for three months. If we married, she could stay; if not, she would have to return to Israel. This seemed like a law made by a bachelor, a sort of trial with a money-back guarantee. I received all the forms and filled them out. Iris, on the other side of the Atlantic, was finding out what she needed to do to be released from the army.

A letter arrived.

Dear Bob,

After our talk last Saturday I went to arrange the thing in the army. So, first thing I want to know agin what happened with the visa. As I understand it, I'll get visa and in three months well get married in US.

I want to know what happened if well get married in Israel. I can arrange a special vacation to come to the states and get marred ther. It will take 2 -3 weeks to arrange this thing and I had to sign in a document that I'll get marred in a short time. Tell me how this arrangement look to you.

Now Bob, I know more or less what I want from life, I mean what I want to study and work after. But I'm sure I don't want to be a housewife that wait to here husband all day for etting deaner together and go to bed. I'm not that type of person and I hope you don't want that type of wife.

Wait for you,
Iris

Reading the letter, I was uneasy that Iris seemed certain we would marry while I was undecided. Even though I had decided to go to Israel, there was still something surreal about the situation. Boy meets girl over a year ago for several weeks, then flies six thousand miles to get married. I had to know more. I had to find out as much as I could before I traveled so far.

In my next phone call to her I asked, "How do I know that you are not marrying me just to come to the US?"

"Do you really feel I leave country and family I love, leave friends and all to come to stay with man I no want? If you think that way, maybe better you not come at all." She hung up.

I felt bad, but I had to make her realize what was on my mind.

Dear Iris,

Please don't be mad for too long. Try not to get upset. Marriage is tough, filled with uncertainties about the one you married. Honesty, loyalty, and love all come into question. Here in Texas, so many girls get married out of high school. They haven't traveled the world like you, but in age, they are the same.

It will be up to both of us to decide whether marrying me would be the best thing for you. I feel you have a maturity equal to women much older that I have dated, but still it will be hard for a girl? woman? of nineteen to come home to the same man each day, to realize that she can't date anymore and must take part of the responsibility of keeping a home. Perhaps that is why so many young women are single and divorced. This is one of the reasons I have not come to see you sooner. This visit will be our only chance to decide. I want you to have all the preparatory time you need to date other men and to think about what you want from life.

Bob

It seemed in every conversation I said the same thing: "Do you know what you're doing, Iris?" She always gave the same answer: "Yes, I want you to come."

After receiving my passport there was nothing left to do except wait until it was time to make my visit. It was November in Odessa, a month before my trip to Israel. You couldn't tell the seasons in Odessa as there weren't any. You had hot weather and hotter weather with a few chilly days they called winter.

As promised, Steven was on his way to Odessa. Just as I was done telling Steven how clear the weather was, a freak winter snowstorm arrived. With the airport closed, a very disgruntled brother arrived from Dallas by bus. I picked him up at the bus station and we drove back to my apartment. It was late, so we prepared to sleep.

"Are you going to Israel to see your honey?" he said, readying his bed on the floor.

I gathered some blankets and a pillow for him. "Yes, I'm going in December, have my tickets and all. I must decide what to do with this girl. I can't keep going on writing and phoning. What do you think?"

Steven layered the floor with blankets to cushion the hard surface. "I can't tell you what to do. I don't know the girl. She's pretty, but that's all I know. You must decide what you want. How do you feel about her?"

How many times had I asked myself the same question? I did a lot of conjecturing but never reached a conclusion. "I don't know. I can talk to her. She seems to really care about me and gives me good advice. But is this love? Am I ready for marriage? Will she be able to live here and be happy if we do marry? So many questions," I replied, more to myself than to Steven.

Steven stopped arranging his blankets and looked directly at me. "Well then, that's what you're going to find out. Just remember one thing: when you get there and spend time with her, don't feel that you're obliged to marry her. If it doesn't feel right, don't do it. You may feel bad taking up her time, but you will be doing yourself and her a big disservice if you marry her out of guilt. Go there and have a good time and let yourself feel what is right. Talk it out, but remember, you're asking a lot from this girl to give up so much to come live with you. Don't take that kind of sacrifice lightly." He returned to his sheets and blankets. "I want to thank you for these luxurious accommodations. I ride through a snowstorm to see my darling brother, who offers me a piece of his floor for a bed."

I did feel a little sorry for him, but just a little. "You could have the bed if you want but seeing as you've done such a remarkable job with the blankets and sheets, I'd hate to take this away from you."

Steven crawled into his bed. "You're not the only one undecided. Nancy and I still want to leave Monticello. It's a real shithole. Remember that new tanning salon they built? Well, it closed in six months. It's just as dirty and rundown as when you were there. If I could find a nice practice and sell mine, I would leave."

Steven had wanted to leave Monticello almost as soon as he arrived. Even when I worked there, he was scouting for opportunities. He had spent many, many hours cursing the place. I asked him why he hadn't left already.

He looked up from the floor. "It's not so easy to leave a practice when you're making a good living. Besides, I thought we would work together, it's what we planned to do. I'm waiting for you before I move. It seems a shame that two brothers in the same field can't get a place to work. There are just too many doctors."

I thought about all the previous problems I'd had working with Steven. I thought about how Iris warned me that I would never be happy working with him. But surely, with my new knowledge, I would garner greater respect from him. I still clung to the belief that things would work out.

Steven was soon asleep, and I went back to my room to think. At least for the present, things were going well. I had a good offer to stay with Dr. Sheets, and later, if I wanted to leave, I could, with three months' notice. I would go to Israel and decide whether to marry Iris. If things didn't work out between us, I would at least get to see Israel. Steven was right. It was asking a lot for such a young girl to come to a new land to live.

I had written so many negative letters to Iris that it was time to set a more conciliatory tone. I wasn't sure I was in love, but I was certain that out of all the women I had dated, she was the one I most wanted.

Dear Iris,

So often I have written to you to try to discourage you from marrying me, but I want to put aside my writing on money, jobs, and education to tell you how I feel. We have spent so little time together, but I can't help admiring you for being willing to give up your lifestyle to live half a world away.

No doubt we will have many difficulties to overcome. You will have to adjust to a new culture. As a young woman, the tedium of being married may not be to your liking. For me, I must learn to understand that not only will I be a husband but a teacher to you as well. Let us realize that no matter how cold life may become, we will have the warmth of each other's love to comfort us.

So often among the problems we forget what brought us together; that is a desire to take one person that can share what you have and make it grow —more laughter, more happiness, more of all the good things that make life worthwhile. I sincerely hope that together we can overcome all obstacles. I hope when we meet that this will be our course, to share our love, remembering that is what is most important in our lives. To make each other happy even if individually we are sad; to care from this day till the last day of our lives.

Bob

I was somehow being drawn into a marriage like a plane on autopilot. It was very frightening to be considering such an important decision with so many unanswered questions.

After sealing and posting the letter, it was late. I had to get up early the next morning for surgery. Steven would be coming to the clinic and to the operating room. I was anxious to show him what I had learned. I would show big brother what I knew, and he didn't.

CHAPTER SEVENTEEN
Bureaucracy

The next morning the sun was out, and the snow was melting. The creaking of wood heralded Steven's awakening. We had breakfast and were soon on the way to the clinic.

Steven watched as Dr. Sheets, and I did several cataract operations. Previously, these surgeries took an hour under general anesthesia, with several days of hospitalization. People had to wear thick "coke bottle" glasses after the operation to see. This new cataract surgery was done under local anesthesia in fifteen minutes. No hospitalization was necessary. And with the insertion of a synthetic lens into the eye, the patient could see with thin or even without glasses. All this was new to Steven, and he took careful notes while watching. At lunch I asked him what he thought.

"You've certainly come a long way in the last few months. Why when you left Monticello you could hardly hold an instrument without shaking all over, and now you're doing surgery even your older brother can't do." He pointed a finger at me. "But remember, no matter how much surgery you know, I'll always be a better businessman. By the way, I don't think you're going to leave here. Dr. Sheets thinks a lot of you; he told me he hoped I wasn't here to take you away. Yes Bob, I think our working together is just a dream."

Steven looked down as a faint smile came across his face. I wasn't sure if it was because he thought our partnership plans were in jeopardy or because his little brother outperformed him in the operating room. "Don't give up. I've made no definite plans that would prevent us from working together in the future. Even if I stay here a brief time, I'm not married to this place."

Steven shook his head. "No, but you'll see that the longer you stay in one place, the harder it is to move. No, I think my young, sophisticated brother is going to be a permanent resident in Odessa."

After lunch we headed back to the office, where Steven practiced surgery in the animal lab while I saw patients in the clinic.

After work, we drove around town, passing a synagogue. "Now Steven, that is a tourist attraction," I said pointing at the building. "This is the only temple for several hundred miles. I think we are an endangered species here. The chances of finding a Jewish girl here are less than finding a tree, and that is low indeed."

It was getting late as we drove up to a local restaurant for dinner.

Steven eyed the women in the restaurant. "I don't know, Bob, the girls in Texas look pretty good to me."

I took a deep breath in and exhaled. "I can't say two words to them. My friends can go up to a girl and say, 'Want to screw?' and be in bed. I'm lucky if I get one dance in before they walk away. I just have nothing in common with these people."

Steven took his eyes off the waitress as she disappeared into the kitchen. "Look, make the best of it while you're here. Ask your friends for some leads. If it's that bad, you may want to move. One piece of advice, when you're in Israel don't marry this girl because you're lonely. If you do, you'll regret it."

I smiled meekly. "No, no. I'm not that stupid. Besides divorces are expensive."

The next few days passed quickly, with Steven continuing to learn new techniques.

It was soon time for him to return to Monticello. As he got ready to board his plane, he again admonished me: "Well, Bob, it was very worthwhile for me. Your brother appreciates it. When you come back from Israel, we'll see you, I hope. Now have a good time and think about what I said. Don't do anything out of guilt or loneliness. Remember if you're not thinking of yourself; think of the girl."

We shook hands, and he was off.

Before I left for Israel, some loose ends needed to be tied up. I signed a contract from Dr. Sheets for an additional year's employment. Iris informed me that it would not be possible for her to leave the country until her army service was over or she married in Israel. I called the US Immigration Services to ask them how to bring over a wife. I had already filled out a multitude of forms for a visa for her to come to the States to marry.

"Well, Dr. Jaffee, this will require new forms to be filled out and filed," the immigration agent said.

I had already gotten writer's cramp from all the previous forms I had filled out. I protested to the agent. "What about all those papers I previously filled out? If they were good enough to bring a woman here for three months who I might marry, aren't they good to bring in a woman I have already married?"

The clerk was nonplussed, calmly stating, "No, I'm sorry. New forms will be required."

I asked when the new forms would be sent as I was leaving for Israel in a few weeks.

"Oh, these forms must be filled out in Israel and filed over there."

Now I lost my composure, raising my voice. "You mean to tell me as an American citizen, I must go to Israel to fill out a form that is to be sent back to the US so they can send me word in Israel that I can take my wife back to America? Do you know how absurd that sounds?"

He told me he would send me the new forms so I could at least look them over, adding have a nice day. Then he hung up.

It would be no easy task, going to Israel. Now I would have ten days in Israel not only to decide if I wanted to get married but also to file the papers and arrange the wedding.

Only a few weeks before my trip, a letter arrived from Iris. Someone must have written it for her, because the English was much improved.

Dear Bob,

It was difficult to tell you everything over the telephone. I suppose I'll just have to wait to see you in December. However, you must understand that 2 or 3 weeks does not really give us much time to discuss things, let alone to make plans.

I want you to understand all the red tape and bureaucratic garbage we have to go through if we decide to marry. First, we have to go to the rabbinate and set a date to be married. It's about a month's wait. Once the date is set, I then tell the army. I must give them about one month's notice. Next, we must go to the American embassy, this I must do with you. I don't know all the details, but I do know that it is very difficult to get a visa and a green card, whether I am married or not. So, I hope you see that there are many problems.

So, when you come in December, you may have to stay longer than 2 or 3 weeks. I cannot do all of this on my own, and there may be a lot of time involved in getting everything done, as you know I've never done this before. We are talking about our future and your boss must understand that you may need more time, that's just the way it is. I am not sure what your plans are like: you will come here and if we decide to marry go back to the US and return at a later date. But if we decide to marry once you're here, we must follow through with it. I must give rabbinate and army exact dates, which, once given, are not easy to change, and there are many things we must do together that will take time.

Bob, since I last saw you, I have been through many changes, some hurtful and some not, and I hope you will not hurt me. It's difficult to explain, but should we decide upon marriage and have to postpone those plans while you go back to the US and return later, it will be unbearable for me to return to my normal routine. I just know that I will feel very let down, so please try to understand this.

Love,
Iris

I didn't understand all that Iris said had to be done if we married. The most important thing was to determine whether we even wanted to marry. The rest I felt would somehow be worked out. I began to pack my bags and get ready for the trip. Along with the clothes, went a mental trunk full of unanswered questions and potential problems.

Will I marry? Will I end the relationship? Was I making a mistake in even going?

Not to mention that the immigration forms never arrived.

CHAPTER EIGHTEEN
Arriving in Israel

*W*ife? *We would have barely ten days together, is that enough time to decide on a lifetime?*

I reviewed in my mind what I knew about Iris, the time in Monticello, the letters, the phone calls. Bits and fragments of a relationship spread over a year and a half. She was intelligent, caring, determined. But what would Iris be like in the US away from her security of family, friends, culture, language?

I flew from Odessa to Dallas and to New York where I boarded the plane for Israel. As I buckled my seat belt I wondered. Would I recognize her? I looked in my wallet for a picture to refresh my memory. As the plane lined up on the runway, I felt my heart was also lining up, both about to leave their base and fly into the unknown. Something was about to happen; good or bad, these next two weeks would be an experience not to forget.

The plane from New York to Israel, which left at 11:00 p.m., was full. Everyone had a piece of their neighbor's elbow. The early excitement faded with the increasing boredom of the thirteen-hour flight. Time was punctuated by meals or a movie. The flight attendants talked among themselves and when interrupted, made you realize the error of your intrusion. I tried several thousand positions to get comfortable and sleep but to no avail. As the first morning light came through the windows, a group of orthodox Jews gathered for morning prayer. They stood, huddled in the back of the plane by the bathroom, dressed in black with their tefillin on their arms, weaving back and forth to the rhythm of the prayers in Hebrew. I was certainly getting nearer to the Jewish state. As the plane approached the Israeli coast the loudspeakers came alive with vibrant Jewish music. My pulse quickened, not only from the music but the expectation of seeing Iris.

Will she be as I remember? Has she changed in appearance? In personality? Will she still care for me as she said? How will I feel when I see her?

It took some time to clear customs. I went into the terminal to claim my baggage, straining to see the face I remembered. Then, among a lengthy line of people waiting, there was one with long blond hair, standing on her tiptoes, waving and yelling "Bob, Bob, Bob." She ran toward me and wrapped her arms around me just as if she left off when we were last together. She kissed and held me and kissed me again. No returning hero could have felt slighted at such a reception.

"Bob, welcome to Israel. My parents over there. I've told them so much about you that they die to meet you. How your flight?" she said, hooking her arm around mine and leading me to greet her parents. Before I could open my mouth, she continued: "Oh, Bob, I can't believe you really here. I never think you really come."

No matter how tiring the flight was, seeing Iris revived me. "It's wonderful to see you. I told you I'd come, and here I am," I said, spreading my arms their full width. I took a step back to look at her. "You're as beautiful as when I last saw you."

We went over to Iris's parents, who introduced themselves as Iris again reached over to hold my arm. She smiled broadly; her "Bob" had finally materialized.

"Mr. and Mrs. Klein, I am so glad to meet you. Iris has told me so much about you," I said, extending my hand. Mr. Klein was about fifty-five years old, tall, broadly built, and slightly bald. Mrs. Klein looked similar in age; she was thin, elegant looking, with short black hair. She smiled slightly, out of courtesy. I didn't think they were happy to see a person from outside Israel come and maybe take their daughter away. However, they were both pleasant. They asked me to call them by their first names, Ziggy and Sarah.

After I reunited with my luggage, Ziggy took charge. His English was much worse than Iris's and even Sarah's. He would ask them both what I had said, and they would tell him in Hebrew. But he eventually found the English to say he would get the car and take us home.

I did not want to inconvenience Iris's parents by depending on their car. I insisted on renting one. Iris's parents argued something in Hebrew. They said they looked forward to talking with me later, kissed Iris and left.

We rented a car that was so minute that I couldn't decide whether to put the luggage in the car or the car in the luggage. However, we squeezed in and were off. I wanted to stop somewhere on the way to her house to talk, and she recommended a café. We drove from Ben Gurion Airport into Tel Aviv, passing three- and four-story buildings with stucco exteriors. Small stores and outdoor cafés lined the wide streets. It had the effect of a large town rather than a big city but then again, I was used to New York City. My first taste of Israeli culture came from the roads. How could so many people be honking their horns at once? I wasn't going to like these people If their personalities matched their aggressiveness and impatience in driving.

It started to rain as we pulled up to the café that Iris had picked. It was December in Tel Aviv, but the temperature was still in the low sixties, so only a jacket was needed. We got out of the car. The café reminded me of Greenwich Village. It was not fancy but was inviting, with a large window that had the name of the establishment in Hebrew. You could see the wooden tables placed close together through the window. There were mostly young people in their twenties, dressed in jeans and casual wear. I felt old at thirty-one.

"This good place. I go once in a while when friend have money to take me," Iris said as we approached the entrance.

I raised my eyebrows. "What do you mean when a friend has money to take you? What friend?"

Iris turned to me and stated calmly. "Well, I not have enough money in army to pay for everything, not even enough to pay for cigarettes, so if I want to go out, I have to have someone take me. See how simple that is."

"These people that take you out and pay for you, they wouldn't happen to be men, would they?"

Iris remained calm. "That really none of your business. Now if you want to stay out here in rain, it okay, but I'm going inside." She turned and disappeared into the café. I didn't want to be left out on the street, and besides, maybe she could get back home without the car, but even with the car I couldn't find my way.

I walked into the café to find Iris sitting at one of the wooden tables. It was a rather small table, and we could easily reach across it to each other. There was little decoration on the cement walls, just the tables crowded together, a counter and young people, sitting, talking, and smoking.

Iris had a menu covering her face and didn't look up as I approached. "Madam, may I sit down or are you saving this seat for someone?"

She looked away from her menu. "Just waiting for a good looking American, one rich enough to pay the bill."

I grabbed the menu from her hands as she started to laugh. She rose partly from the table to kiss me and whispered. "You're not so handsome, nor so rich, but you American and only one in room." She threw her arms around me and enveloped me in kisses.

"Iris, easy, people will be looking at us. I don't want to be the entertainment for the place," I said as I tried to hold her back.

"Oh, Bob, nobody care," she said returning to her seat.

The waitress was standing by the table tapping her pencil on a pad and looking impatient. We gave her our order. While waiting, I pulled out some photos. Taken just outside of Odessa, they showed the city from a distance.

I handed the pictures to her. She looked at each of them for a second before declaring, "Bob, you sure these pictures developed? I no see nothing on them."

I took the photos. "What? Let me see." I didn't see anything that was wrong as I handed the photos back to her. "There's not a whole lot to see."

"That's it?" Iris shrieked. "Bob, is this a joke? You tell me that is place you think I want to live? Bob, you crazy?"

The smile fell from my face. "Now don't get so upset," I said, picking out one of the photos. "See, this line is the horizon. It's very flat, and those little bumps are buildings. They're not very tall but there are a lot of them. Odessa has tens of thousands of people."

She took the photo, looked at it again, "It still look to me like a person's face that have pimples." She threw the photo on the table.

"How is the army?" I said as I put the photos away.

"Army terrible. I have good job and get to travel all around with important men, but it still terrible. I hate it. Last week I get to go with general all around country as he make tour of bases. I sit and listen to his problems with wife. He trust me a lot," Iris said.

"How could you hate the army? You get to travel around with generals all over the place. It sounds like a vacation! By the way how did you manage to get these two weeks off to be with me?"

Iris sat up in the chair and swung her long blond hair out of the way. "Bob, army no vacation! People just happen to like me 'cause I good listener. It not easy to get time off. Lot of people no like me 'cause they think I get too much vacation." She smiled. "But it good to be liked by important people, it make things easier."

"How could you, a nineteen-year-old private, become the confidant of so many important people? Are you sure you're not sleeping with the leadership of the Israeli army?"

Iris rose half out of her chair as if to leave, her hair trailing in the breeze of her movement. "I no understand all of that but the part about the bed I know. What you think, I whore? You not very nice. It's not true and it hurt you think that way about me." She fell back in her seat and looked down into her lap. The rain was falling outside, tears inside.

I knew I had made a mistake accusing her of sleeping around. It was stupid of me, yet I still wasn't sure how she managed the extra perks. I apologized and reached across the table to pick up her head, holding it steady as I kissed her lips. She pulled back and wiped some tears forming in her eyes. The waitress stood watching with the coffee and pastry in hand and curtly asked me in English if we were ready to be served. I thought between the waitress and the drive into Tel Aviv, Israelis were a difficult people to like. The waitress plunked the coffee on the table spilling a good part into my lap. I reached for a napkin.

Wiping away the coffee from my pants I paused for a few seconds. Looking back at Iris I changed the topic of conversation.

"Where should we go for the next two weeks? I would like to see Jerusalem and Masada and travel around a bit. What do you think?" I asked cheerfully.

Iris dried her tears and composed herself. "First, you must spend time with my parents. They hear so much about you for whole year now they want to meet you. I think it be no trouble to travel around, but really it not very interesting."

"What do you mean, uninteresting? There is so much history here, how can it be boring?" I said.

Iris yawned. "It all look alike. Lots of old rocks, everything old rocks. I live here all my life and I tired of seeing old rocks. Now I think it much better if we go and see lots of movies and go out to dinner. What you think about that?"

"I'm not sure I came six thousand miles to see movies in Hebrew," I said trying again to remove the coffee stains from my pants.

"Oh, don't worry, the movies are in English, so you have no trouble understand them," she assured me. I still hadn't come so far to see movies in Hebrew or English.

I decided to compromise, telling her that during the day we would go where I wanted and, in the evening, where she wanted. She agreed.

The itinerary decided, I braved the ire of the Israeli drivers and drove to Iris's house for the evening. As I drove, I didn't know what I would say to Iris's parents. I wasn't sure Iris and I would get married, but I was sure they could not be happy about her dating an American.

CHAPTER NINETEEN
Israel

*W*e arrived at Iris's house. It was in a residential neighborhood of similar-looking homes. They were all one-story poured concrete, with a small patch of grass in front. Iris's house had an outer layer of cement over the concrete that was textured with vertical wavy lines. An inlaid stone walkway of varying shapes led to the entrance. The interior walls were of cement—no wood or wallboard.

I greeted her parents, and we gathered for the evening meal. It was strange to be sitting at a table with a lot of noise I couldn't understand. Also unfamiliar to me was the light evening fare, sauces white and tan, pita bread, and salad. I could understand the bread and salad but needed Iris to explain the hummus and tahini sauces. It soon occurred to all present, when I didn't pass the salt, that I didn't understand a word of Hebrew. As difficult as English was for them, they would stumble but still make themselves understood. They asked me about my trip, about Texas, and my work. I believe Sarah and Ziggy were trying to determine what Iris saw that was so special in me that it couldn't be duplicated in an Israeli. I started to fall asleep at dinner; the seven-hour time difference and being up for over twenty-four hours was catching up to me. Fearing I would fall and drown in the hummus Iris took me to a room that felt like a concrete bunker and I was soon asleep.

* * *

The next morning gave me more opportunities to observe the family. Noah, being two, was the easiest to know. Two-year-olds seem to have a universal personality deeply rooted in shyness with liberal doses of rambunctiousness. Alina, thirteen, was quiet, with a delightful smile that made you wonder what she was really thinking. Ziggy impressed me as a father with the way he weaved from sternness to softness, listening, planning, and ordering as he went about being the head of the house. There was no doubt about his concern for his family—he noted where everyone was, when anything needed to be done, and who was to do it. But if Ziggy was concerned with the mechanical operations of the family, the spiritual leadership belonged to Sarah. She set the mood. Her quietness contrasted with the commotion around her. This lady gave her orders in silence. A look, a gesture, was sufficient. Her conversations were held with family members quietly in corners—no arguing, no haggling.

On my first day in Israel, we went to Caesarea. Ziggy arranged the trip and was as good a tour guide as his English would allow. He explained how Herod the great had built the town, named for the Roman emperor Caesar Augustus. The town was once a great port. We toured the stone amphitheater that abutted the Mediterranean. He pointed out the stone aqueduct that brought water in. I marveled at the ingenuity and architectural beauty of the arches. Iris leaned on my shoulder, whispering for me to just listen and follow her father. The weather was beautiful, with bright sun and temperatures of about seventy.

It was wonderful, but I came to Israel to decide my future. Traveling with the family didn't seem conducive to having intimate conversations with Iris.

That evening at Iris's house I insisted that we travel for a few days by ourselves. Ziggy understood; he took out a map to show us how to go to Jerusalem.

* * *

The next morning found Iris and me on the road. As we drove up the mountains to Jerusalem, I again asked Iris about her thoughts on marriage.

"Bob, I not know. It very difficult thing to decide. We have time now to think. I don't feel it enough time, but we must make choice. If we decide to get married and have to put it off I no think I go on."

I continued to probe, asking her how she would feel about leaving her family, school, about being a wife. I glanced toward her as I tried to keep the toy car on the road. She moved closer to me and put her arm around my shoulder.

She spoke softly. "How I able to know all you ask? I do what I feel is best, but how I able to be sure until I try? If we try and it no work than only thing to do is get divorce. I maybe want to try to be actor in school, maybe I do it, maybe not, but I want to go to school and be something. I feel all this time that I want you and I no change my mind but maybe as I get to know you more, I no want you. I can only do what I feel at this time to be good. I no know what happen years from this time."

There was such simplicity yet logic in her answer. She had distilled a complex situation from its myriad of parts.

"You ask me how I be in place I never see. I only say I do best I can and hope all be okay, more than that I can no promise," she said.

When I again asked her if she had at least thought about all I had asked she took her hand from my shoulder and turned to look out the window.

As if she was talking to herself, she said, "I think very much about all you say, it is not new to me. It my life, you think I want to throw it away? I try. I try to do what it be to have success. Maybe with your help I make it and we be very happy. More than that I not know."

I was looking for definite answers, and she was smart enough to know the future has no definite promises.

The car crawled its way up to Jerusalem. Everywhere I looked, things were growing: bananas, oranges, grapes. There were many other plants I couldn't identify. Astonished, I blurted out, "In Hebrew school they told me Israel was a desert."

Iris started to laugh. "Bob, sometimes you big idiot. This country always desert. The mountains have no trees until we plant them. All the trees you see we plant one by one. When I little I used to plant trees. Now you wait, I show you something else. Soon we pass old broken-down trucks from 1948 war. They put them there to remind people of the fight."

As promised, around the next curve in the road were the burned remains of military vehicles. I was fascinated by the history and eagerly turned to my guide to explain more.

"What you want me to say? These old broken trucks hit by Arabs. They look to me like other broken trucks—these trucks just more famous."

I objected to her blasé attitude. There must be more to the story.

She responded puffing out a breath of air: "Of course, I learn about this in school. I learn about it for fourteen years. It no make difference every little thing. These still old trucks that get hit in war and no work anymore."

There was no doubt Iris and I had a different appreciation of history. I didn't want to tell her my hobby was collecting American Civil War artifacts. She would never understand why.

We soon approached the old city of Jerusalem. There on top of a mountain was this fortress in varying shades of tan. Built with large blocks of stone was a wall completely enclosing the city, save for several entry gates. I parked the car in one of the lots just outside the walled city.

As we walked up to one of the gates, I could see slits in the rocks for pouring hot oil on invaders or shooting arrows. How incongruous this was, mixing with the pockmarks of modern automatic weapons on the same rocks.

The inside of the city was crisscrossed with narrow alleys and streets. Because the streets were so narrow, only donkeys could be used for transport. Everything was stone. The buildings, the streets, the stairs, all stone. Vendors with loaves of freshly baked bread on their shoulders hurried to their destinations. Other vendors seemed to hide in the crevices awaiting the chance to extol their merchandise to a passing tourist. There were kiosks selling dresses, leather bags, brass objects, and souvenirs; and fresh food markets with hanging butchered meat. We strolled the stone streets as old women wearing headdresses, called hijab, and black robes, called abaya, knelt to offer fruit or other produce for sale. Nestled into the walls were small coffee shops. Arab men, with their traditional headdresses, called keffiyeh, sat apathetically smoking water pipes or drinking coffee. As we entered and exited dimly lit, arched stone tunnels, we passed orthodox Jews in black dress. We saw a few Greek orthodox monks in their black robes and kalimavkion headdress. I was soon lost. But Iris had no trouble navigating having been here many times before. Her stoic manner contrasted with my enthusiasm as I strained my neck trying to take all these strange sights in. It looked to me like Disneyland on steroids. But it was all real.

Iris found a vendor selling falafel, and as this was one of her favorite foods, we had to get some.

"Falafel, Iris, is this Israeli or imported American?" I teased.

"Bob, it neither, it Arab. You forget I tell you that in America. Now come with me and I show you," Iris said as she started to bargain with the vendor. I was continuing my education in falafel. I could now eat it without sharing it with my clothes. The white sauce, called tahini, was made from sesame seeds. The warm pita bread was stuffed with fried chickpeas or eggplant, I wasn't sure. It was covered with green vegetable salad, plenty of garlic, and tahini, so if I couldn't exactly see what I was eating I could taste it. It was delicious.

We walked toward the Jewish quarter of Jerusalem filled with orthodox Jews in their black dress, fur hats, beards, and tefillin. They had come to pray at the Wailing Wall. This comprised the remnants of the outer wall from the second temple destroyed by the Romans. Looking at it, I couldn't help remembering my cousin's remark that it reminded him of the back of Yankee Stadium. It was not very impressive, a wall of large stone blocks. Guarding the wall at the top was an Israeli soldier armed with a machine gun. The men and women were separated in different sections to pray and place notes between the rocks. These notes were to be read by God. The chanting of the many, black-robed men against the wall, the earnestness of their prayers, the back-and-forth weaving and concentration as they prayed conveyed the importance of this site.

Just beyond the Wailing Wall was the golden Dome of the Rock, built in the seventh century, where the prophet Muhammad is said to have ascended to heaven. The location was easily visible from the glistening sunlight off its roof. It is on the al-Haram-al-Sharif, al-Aqsa Mosque compound, or the Temple Mount, where the Temple of Jerusalem once stood. The site has major significance to both the Islamic and Jewish religions.

It was getting toward sunset as we started back. An Arab vendor came out of the shadows selling traditional Arab headdress, the keffiyeh. I didn't know what I was going to do with it in Texas but thought it would be a nice souvenir.

"Twenty-five shekels, very cheap, try it on," the vendor beckoned.

"I will give you twenty shekels for it," I said trying to show what an experienced haggler I was.

Iris looked at me in disbelief. "What? You crazy, it not worth five shekels for this piece of junk but you be here all day. Get out of my way. I tell him."

Iris started talking to the vendor in Hebrew. Gesticulating, raising her voice, and finally pulling me away, she cajoled him to drop the price to fifteen shekels. She took my prize and dumped it into my hands as she admonished, "Here, now you got this piece of junk but at least it not cost you all your money. What are you going to do with it? Bob, I think maybe you lose your head." She started to laugh, pulling me down the street, shielding me from the other vendor vultures who, smelling tourists, surrounded us selling everything from pieces of the original cross to a freshly killed chicken. As they approached, she would yell something at them in Hebrew and they would retreat.

I was awed by the way Iris protected me from the zealous merchants. She was a real "sabra," tough on the outside, soft on the inside.

The sun was setting behind the old city walls. It was time to leave Jerusalem and find a hotel room for the evening. I put my arm around her and kissed her.

There is much to like in this woman. Is this what love feels like? I just don't know.

CHAPTER TWENTY
Decision Made

After we checked in at the hotel, I was faced with keeping my agreement with Iris to go to the movies. I still hated sitting for two hours watching movies, especially in a foreign language, but a promise is a promise.

Before entering the theater, we were frisked for weapons. This was normal for Israel, a country constantly at war. I slept through most of the movie and didn't recall anything about it except that it ended. Thank God!

After the movie we walked around the subdued, tree-lined streets and found a Chinese restaurant for dinner. Fortunately, the menu was in Hebrew and English, so we both could order. Neither of us knew what the other had requested.

After having the soup Iris felt ill, feeling slightly nauseous. We headed back to the hotel, one arm holding Iris, the other several pounds of Chinese food.

After she had a short nap and felt better, we opened the now cold containers of food.

"This very good choice, it must be what I ordered," Iris said with a blink of her eyes.

I tweaked Iris's thigh. The container of fried rice she was holding tilted, depositing some of its contents on the bed. Iris brushed the bed to clear some of the rice off as we laughed.

We were both feeling relaxed, and I took the opportunity to again quiz Iris on her future. I was not very discreet when I asked her why she thought she loved me.

Iris put down her container of food on the side table and let out a sigh. "I think you most honest man I ever meet. You remind me of my father. Maybe I wrong but I in love with you." She threw her arms around me. "I love you, but I no feel that you love me. If you don't, say now, it better than if you say later."

Looking away from her I slowly cleared the bed of all the remaining cartons of food. "What makes you think I don't love you?" My attention was drawn to a spot of food on the sheets.

"I just feel it so. Maybe you here 'cause you have no one else. Maybe you feel that since you here you have to marry me. I really not know why you here or what you think," she said, taking her arms away from me, leaning back in bed, and letting her head fall to her chest.

I cleaned the spot of food from the bed and had a drink of water. It seemed like an eternity passed in silence. I moved closer to her and tried to put my arms around her, but she pushed away.

"No, no, you tell me in words what you think," she demanded.

I thought carefully about how to reply. I moved back from her and took another sip of water. Carefully I placed the cup on the table. The tops of the food containers were open, so I slowly closed each one of them. Iris just sat silently with her head bowed, looking down at her hands.

"Iris, it's not that I have no one else. It would be very stupid for me to come here just to go to bed with you. I wouldn't marry you unless I loved you. It would be a lot of problems for the both of us if we broke up later. There are just some things that I want to be sure of, that I need the next few days to find out."

"What you not sure of? Tell me."

"I still don't know if you could make it in Texas. In my own mind I don't know if you are marrying me just for money. I am not—"

Iris waved her hand in front of my face and shouted: "Stop, stop. We gone over this thousand times. If you think you get answer in few days maybe better you take me home now." She turned away and buried her head in the pillow.

I picked up her head, smoothed away the hair from her face. She didn't want to look at me, but I held her, firmly looking into her eyes. I don't know what made me realize my answer. It occurred so instantaneously. Yes, she was smart, attractive, ambitious, and had a sense of humor. She would listen to my problems and give mature advice. And most important, she really loved me. I just could not say goodbye to something this wonderful. But I wasn't sitting there with paper and pen checking off the boxes. I guess love is not a science paper of proven conclusions. Maybe love is what Iris said it was, something that just <u>feels</u> right. You can't put it into words. My heart was satisfied and superseded any lingering questions in my mind. *This is the woman I want as my wife. I can't leave her behind.*

"Iris, I love you. I don't know what the years will hold but if you're willing to try, I want you to be my wife," I said softly, continuing to look straight into her eyes.

She threw her arms around me, whispering how much she loved me. Tears formed in her eyes. The decision had been made.

CHAPTER TWENTY-ONE
Making Plans

The next morning, Iris was quick to start planning. "There is no time to waste. We have many things to do if we are to marry. First, we must go to Rabbinate and arrange wedding. Then I must go to army and get release. Then we must go to US consulate and get form for me to come to US. So, you see it no easy what we plan to do, and it take much time. We must hurry if we to get everything done in two weeks. If I tell army I want to leave to marry an American and I don't get married it will be very hard on me, so you must not lie to me and leave me here and go back to States without me. Bob, I hope you mean what you say. I love you so much, it kill me if you say nice things to me just to cheer me up."

I smiled. "For a guy you called the most honest man you ever met, I must be slipping, or else the guys you met before were criminals." I stopped smiling and looked directly at her. "I love you. That is why I want you to be my wife—for that reason and no other. I'm not here to try to fool you. I came because I wanted to know if you are the woman to be with for the rest of my life. I believe I have made the right choice. Now, enough!"

I felt I had allayed her fears when she embraced me. She tightened her grip on my neck. I couldn't be sure if it was love or if she was trying to strangle me. I guessed it was the former.

We had a quick breakfast in Jerusalem and headed back to Tel Aviv to begin the marital process.

Arriving in Tel Aviv Iris's parents were surprised by our one-day trip to Jerusalem because they thought we would be gone for a week.

I retreated to my room to unpack. I took my time as I didn't want to face Sarah and Ziggy with the decision Iris and I had made. This would no doubt be very disappointing to them. Maybe it would ease their minds to know how much I loved Iris and intended to take care of her. But I was sure nothing I could possibly say would relieve the loss of her leaving for the United States.

When I entered the living room, I could tell Iris had told them the news. Sarah stood in the kitchen making dinner, staring out into the distance while her hands worked automatically. Ziggy called me over to talk. His demeanor was entirely business. He communicated to me that in the morning we would go to the Rabbinate to make the necessary arrangements for marriage. With that done he announced dinner would be ready in an hour and suggested a nap in the interim.

I took hold of Iris, and we went to lie down. She snuggled up to me in the bed and intertwined herself within me. From her parents' attitude I knew the answer, I still had to ask how her parents took the news.

Iris was solemn. "They understand why you come here. They not happy I marry you. They wish I marry man from Israel. But they know I love you very much and they no want to stay in way of my happiness. They great parents. They very great people. It hurt them very much that I leave them to go to US, but they don't stop me from going."

At dinner that evening, Sarah spent most of her time studying her plate. She would occasionally ask us what we had done in Jerusalem or what we intended to do next. The answers seemed to ride over her as she bowed her head, staring down at the table.

Ziggy reiterated the plans to visit the Rabbinate in the morning. He would come with us to help. Iris held on to me under the table as we discussed the business of marriage arrangements. It was uncomfortable for what was not said. There was no offer of congratulations, no hugs or handshakes, no welcome to the family.

* * *

The next morning, we were on the way to the Rabbinate. I had no idea what a Rabbinate was and the small white house we stopped at gave no clue. In Israel, Jewish marriages had to be approved by this religious council before they could proceed.

We entered a little waiting room attended by a short middle-aged man who stopped cleaning to ask what business we had. Everything was spoken in Hebrew, so it was difficult for me to follow the conversation without Ziggy or Iris explaining it to me in English. Ziggy, after several minutes of discussion, turned toward us and told us to sit down and wait for the Rabbi. He told me not to worry, that he would answer all the questions in Hebrew for me, and it would be a simple matter. After a half hour wait, we were ushered into the Rabbi's chambers. It felt like entering a time capsule several centuries old. An old man in black attire, black wide-brimmed hat, and a long white beard was sitting hunched over a bare table, save for a few books. The room was stark, with only the walls of bookcases filled with ledgers as a distraction. When the Rabbi rose to greet us, his back was parallel to the ground. His posture seemed frozen. He shook my hand and said something in Hebrew, which I took to be hello. We sat down and Ziggy proceeded to explain our visit. By the fluctuations of their voices up and down and the throwing up of hands, I gathered that the talk had reached an impasse. Ziggy turned toward me and said I would have to prove to the Rabbinate I was Jewish and single. I would need a paper from the States attesting to this. Ziggy suggested that maybe my parents could get my Bar Mitzvah certificate. I felt like shaking the Rabbi by his beard, but I didn't think that would prove I was Jewish and single.

"You mean I came all this way to marry Iris and now I must go back and get this ridiculous piece of paper before we can get married? What difference does it make? I just want to get married," I said to Ziggy.

Ziggy should have been a diplomat. His demeanor was expressionless. "Now, this only way. You need paper, so we will get paper."

Iris listened to the discussion. She threw some words at the Rabbi. By her intonation I could assume that these were not words of agreement. The Rabbi said some words back, got up, shook hands with Ziggy and showed us to the door. Leaving the building, Iris and Ziggy were behind me talking angrily.

Iris moved closer to me. "Bob, this all junk, a lot of junk. Now we not able to get married."

Ziggy was, as usual, the voice of reason. "Now Bob, you and Iris listen. This must be done. You go back, get paper, and then we have marriage. Iris have to wait, there no choice. Iris no like it but will get over it."

I tried to reassure her. "As soon as I return to Texas, I will work on getting the papers. Believe me, Iris, I'm not going to leave you; believe me, I will be back."

"It take you so long to get here, now that you go away you not come back. I sure of it," she replied.

I grabbed her hand and held her back as Ziggy walked on. I picked up her head and forced her to look at me. In a firm and deliberate tone I said, "Stop it. I told you I want you as my wife, and I told you I'm going to return. Stop telling me I won't. Now, I don't want to hear any more doubts. Okay?" I felt strangely calm. I had made the biggest decision of my life, to marry; the rest were technicalities we would overcome.

Iris was not so sure. She just shrugged her shoulders, turned, and walked to the car.

CHAPTER TWENTY-TWO
Leaving

Since nothing further could be done, my remaining time in Israel was spent sightseeing. We went back to Jerusalem. We again strolled through the old walled city. We saw a bunch of air force cadets also enjoying the sites. Iris pointed out that most would never graduate due to the strenuous mental and physical demands.

The courtyard of the Wailing Wall again grabbed my attention. So many people praying in front of a stone wall. Was there really something powerful about this piece of stone, something more than one could see? Neither Iris nor I was deeply religious but if so many attached such significance to these rocks a tourist must at least pay it some respect. I wrote down on a slip of paper my desire for a long and happy marriage. Turning to Iris, I told her I was going up to the wall to pray. I asked if she wanted to go to the women's section to pray.

"No, this all a bunch of junk. I no believe in this. I no know why all these people come here. It seem like a waste of time. You go, I wait," she said.

I walked up to the wall and stood with the other men. They chanted in Hebrew from their prayer books with their ritual shawls, called tallits, over their heads. I did not know any prayers in Hebrew but felt if there was a God, he'd probably understand English. Amongst all the black clad orthodox worshippers me in my blue jeans was also beseeching G-d. I slipped my paper into a crack in the wall asking for a happy and long marriage, my head bowed, leaning against the stones silently I prayed for our union. Within five minutes I rejoined Iris. That evening it was back to another movie to sleep through.

The following day we traveled to Masada. This is where Jewish zealots held out against Roman legions until, when faced with certain capture, they all committed suicide. Herod built this desert retreat on top of a mountain. Water from infrequent rainfall was stored in cisterns. Enough water could be collected in one downfall to last a couple of years, enough even for baths. You could look down from the top of the mountain and see where the Roman camps had been. It was only when the Romans built a ramp going to the top of the mountain that the zealots took drastic action to avoid becoming slaves. I stopped at the remains of the stone houses still present to read the guidebook's explanation of each house. My grumpy companion reiterated her belief that if you've seen one rock, you've seen them all.

That evening, at the hotel near Masada, we watched the sun set over the Dead Sea toward Jordan. Israel is a small country, but the diversity of its mountains, cities, deserts, and, most of all, its people give it an excitement far beyond its size.

As we held hands, gazing, I again asked Iris what she did in the army. Forgetting her vow of secrecy, she was forthcoming. "I do many things, I social worker first. I go to many bases to listen to problems of soldiers. It terrible job. I see many soldiers with big problems 'cause they not able to take it in army. I mostly go to officers' bases where they train very hard. Many of them not able to do it. Some kill themselves 'cause they not able to take the training. It very sad. I ask to transfer and now have very good job in drawing. It very good job, many women want it, but I still hate army very much."

I had no conception of what army life was like.

"No, Bob, you can't know unless you in army. The army no care about the men. They treat them badly to make them tough, but some not able to stand it. I have good friend who kill himself 'cause he not able to take it. I no like to take orders and sometimes get into trouble. It good for me that big officers like me, otherwise I maybe in jail. But many big officers like me and protect me."

"I don't know, Iris, if all those big, important officers like you, you must be very intelligent."

Iris turned toward me and released my hand. "Of course, I intelligent. If you not know by now, than you very stupid."

She wasn't angry very long as she quickly changed the subject worrying about what she would do in Texas. "We will try to get you into school, and you'll get a job, learn how to drive, and be my wife," I said.

"I hope I able to do those things and not just be wife. I want to study very much but it not easy for me not knowing English well," she said softly.

I felt it would be extremely hard for Iris, but I didn't want to upset her before she even arrived in the States. "It won't be easy, but you'll do it, especially since you told me how intelligent you are. If you can sit with the big generals, you can sit with a book. Besides, I don't know how long we will be in Texas. I'm thinking of working with Steven."

Iris exploded like a firecracker going off, moving back from me. "Oh, Bob, you must not do that. You must not go in with brother. You not be happy. Remember how you with brother before, how unhappy you were? Now it not good you in with brother. Listen to me. I want you to be something, to be something on your own. I want you to be something good. I know that you can, you smarter than brother, you better trained than brother, so you not need him to make it. Now Bob, if you go in with brother you never be man of yourself. If you do that I no think that I able to stay with you."

I was sure that, when Iris came to the States and saw the situation, knew Steven a little better, she would acquiesce to us working together.

For the present there was no point in arguing. I defused the topic by stating we would determine our future when the both of us were back in Texas.

On the drive back to Tel Aviv we passed the omnipresent soldiers who lined the highways. Since military conscription was mandatory in Israel, all citizens between age eighteen and twenty-one were in the army. Iris explained that most soldiers had no cars as they were young and, unlike in the United States, few could afford automobiles. Most soldiers traveled by hitching rides. We picked up two soldiers, who happily got into our micro car. They weighed about 170 pounds each, which almost caused the front end of the car to lift off the ground. Soldiers carried their weapons with them wherever they went. Our hitchhikers rested their machine guns across the front seat, one barrel pointed at my right ear, one at my left ear. I prayed we didn't hit a bump.

* * *

Two weeks is not infinite, even if you are forced to make lifelong decisions within that period. The time had come for me to return to Texas. I said my goodbyes to the family. At the airport I wanted one final photo of Iris. It was a damp, rainy day. Iris was dressed in a long, ill-fitting, crimson coat that seemed to gobble her up. She stood outside the terminal building in the light drizzle, impatiently waiting for me to take the picture.

"Hurry up, hurry up," she barked.

I barely had time to focus on the picture. Through the viewfinder was the image of a young woman, sad expression, slumped shoulders, coat too large, and slightly out of focus. I snapped the shutter. Then one more kiss, one more goodbye, and I was off, back to the United States.

CHAPTER TWENTY-THREE
Back in Texas

It was the end of December. Back in Texas I went to work getting the necessary paperwork showing I was Jewish. Fortunately, my parents in New York were able to secure the documents of my Bar Mitzvah, which they sent to Israel.

Iris and I were in close telephone contact about the upcoming wedding.

"Bob, it necessary that we set date for marriage now. We have to decide weeks in advance of when we get married. If we don't give notice now, then we have to wait until after Passover," she said.

"Why do we have to wait until after Passover? Can't we get married in April?"

Israel had rules that were anchored in the Jewish religion. "It not possible to get married during Passover. We either get married in March or wait until May. I no want to wait so long. I want you to come now!"

"I just got back from Israel a week ago. I can't just leave again on a minute's notice," I said.

Iris was adamant. "This is marriage we talk about, this most important thing in your life. You tell boss that you have to go get married."

I didn't think the responsibility I had to my patients allowed me to keep taking time off. Would Dr. Sheets even allow me to leave again so soon? Realistically I could try for another two weeks off at the end of March. I told Iris to arrange the wedding for that time.

This still did not appease her. "What you mean? This very important, you make time. It going to take me maybe weeks to get papers ready and you must be there."

"It's not possible for me to stay for weeks. I am going to come and marry you, and then you can get the papers filed and then join me," I said.

"I not able to come unless I have papers and you will have to be there, you can't just come and leave me behind."

She had a point, but I also felt a responsibility towards my work. "I'm not leaving you behind, but I can't lose my job either. I want you to arrange as much as possible before I get there, so all I will have to do is sign the needed papers."

I could feel the desperation in her voice. "Bob, you make it very difficult for me. I try, but maybe it not possible. It not fair that you leave everything to me. I don't think I can do it. You must stay longer. No argument about this. This your marriage now—you will have to find the time."

Iris was young and had never had a job; how could she understand? Or maybe it was me who didn't understand. "We will do the best we can. Now, the papers for the Rabbinate have been sent. You let me know when the marriage date is, and I will take off the time, but I can't take weeks off. I will see if there is anything here I can do to speed things up."

There was a pause, and then she said softly, "Bob, you love me?"

I laughed to myself. "Iris, would I go through this for somebody I hate?"

"Bob, I love you."

I don't know how many times I needed to reassure her, but I could understand how difficult it must have been for her to make so many arrangements on the conditions I had outlined.

Back at the office I told the staff about my upcoming marriage in Israel. They thought it was some prearranged affair done by my parents, according to Jewish custom. I tried to explain my parents had nothing to do with the marriage and neither did Jewish custom. I told them that if my mother ever arranged for me to marry somebody, it would be the very last person on earth I would marry. Dr. Sheets, to my surprise, was very understanding when I told him my predicament and the need for me to take more time off in March. So at least my job was safe. I tried to expedite matters by hiring an attorney to help me navigate the multitude of forms and speed up the process. After several days of studying the matter, he got back to me.

"Dr. Jaffee, I don't know if there is anything I can do. To tell you the truth, it is easier if you bring your wife into the country illegally and then we can worry about how to keep her here. This would be a lot simpler than trying to get this paperwork figured out. I checked on some of the documents you asked about, and indeed they do have to be signed in Israel."

This was less than a satisfying answer. "I don't think I can just get married in Israel and put my new bride in a wooden crate to the US. Somehow, I think she would be annoyed if I travel first class and she's in baggage."

I was rapidly running out of ideas. I called US Immigration Services in El Paso. They were, as before, helpful in supplying me with all the paper I could possibly use in two lifetimes. However, except for reading me a litany of rules and procedures, they said there was nothing they could do in the States.

The next week I called Iris to tell her about my lack of accomplishments in speeding up the paperwork.

Iris was livid. "Now, you listen to me. I try and go to embassy. They tell me you have to fill out forms in person. Also, you not able to fill out form until after we married and I not able to get release from army until after we married, it take a few days. You can't leave, or you have to come back again 'cause I not able to get everything done."

"Iris, we will get it done, 'cause that is all the time I can spend in Israel."

"It not possible, "she shouted.

I reassured Iris it would be possible but having never done this before and not sure what the forms entailed, I wasn't sure myself. I inquired if Iris had set a wedding date so I could finalize my trip.

"Yes, I have date. March 30. Now, after I set everything up, it be very bad if you no come. I never see friends again if you no come."

I reassured her once again that I would be there and that I loved her, and we hung up. I felt uneasy about accomplishing all that Iris said had to be done if we were to marry in the time I had allotted for my trip. But there was nothing more to be done except fly to Israel, sign every empty form the US embassy had and hope for the best. My parents called to wish me luck on the marriage. They had never seen Iris, nor had I told them much about her. They and my brother congratulated me as they really had little choice.

So, armed with a suitcase full of ballpoint pens, it was back to Israel.

CHAPTER TWENTY-FOUR
Return to Israel

*I*t was March 1981, ten months since I had left Monticello, twenty-one months since I had met Iris. As promised, I returned to Israel to finalize the documents and marry Iris. There was no loss of enthusiasm in Iris's eyes when I arrived. She jumped up and down a little less, but her smile was broader. She hugged me and poured kisses over every part of my face.

"Bob, I so glad you come, now we have much to do. We must go to embassy right away and get papers so I can go to army, and we can get married," Iris said excitedly as she grabbed my arm and pulled.

"Do I get time to get my luggage, or should I just leave it at the airport?" I asked as she dragged me away.

"No be funny, this is serious. You only here for short time. I hope we able to do all these things. Otherwise, you no go home," Iris said letting go of my arm, stopping and looking directly at me.

Iris had arranged for the wedding to be in ten days. The Rabbinate had cleared us to marry after receiving proof that I was Jewish. Now we had to go to the US embassy and file the forms for Iris to obtain visa entry into the States. After we got married Iris could obtain a release from the army. After all this, she would be able to come to the States. But I only had twelve days before returning. Maybe I wasn't being realistic, but I didn't feel filling out the needed forms would take a long time. I was still afraid that taking additional time off would jeopardize my job. My plan was to finish the paperwork, get married, and go back alone. Iris could finish her army release and then join me in Texas.

"Well, let's get going, or I may end up only half married to you," I said with a smile. Iris didn't laugh.

We picked up my luggage and greeted Ziggy, who was waiting at the airport to take us directly to the US embassy.

We waited in line to get into the embassy. I asked how many of the forms she had completed before my visit. She told me she hadn't done any because the forms were in English, and she had trouble understanding them.

"You mean you waited for me before you filed any of these forms? Are you crazy? You could have done this work without me. Now we will never be able to complete these documents. Why didn't you get someone to help you with your English? You mean to tell me there is no one in Israel that speaks and writes English? I don't understand why you don't take care of some things yourself," I said, raising my voice.

"Bob, not so excited. We take care everything. We are here, relax, things will come. Just be calm," Ziggy pleaded, gesticulating with his hands for me to lower my voice.

As the line moved at the rate of one person per infinity, I wasn't sure we would accomplish anything except exercising our shoes. But after several hours, we got inside the embassy, which enabled us to place ourselves on wooden benches for several more hours. The clerk stood behind an iron grating protected by a US Marine. After watching her serve up huge stacks of papers to each applicant I could understand why she needed protection.

"Are all these people waiting just to go to the US?" I said, looking at the long lines.

"Yes, they want to go to US, but they have long wait—it take years. I hope I able to come to US after I marry. I no want to wait in Israel alone for years," Iris answered.

I was thinking that maybe I hadn't realized how difficult this process was. I joked to Iris that if she had to remain in Israel, she had my permission to go out with other men.

I received a soft punch to my arm as Iris responded that it was not funny.

"Don't worry. At the present rate we'll probably both die together on these benches waiting," I said trying to lighten the mood.

We watched as the people went up to the iron grating upon the calling of their number. By the inflection of their voices in Hebrew and their cursing in English it seemed most people were unprepared to write novels to get their visas. Iris and Ziggy just sat there, Iris fidgeting with her clothes, not saying anything as I cursed softly to myself. Finally, just before starvation set in, our number was called. I rushed to the iron grating to present my case.

"My name is Robert Jaffee, and this is my fiancée, Iris. We are going to get married in a few days. She is an Israeli citizen, and I am a US citizen. I want to bring her to the US after our marriage."

After a prolonged yawn the clerk pulled, with surgical skill, various assortments of papers.

"Okay, Jaffee," the clerk began. "You take these forms, you fill them out, and bring them back as soon as you can, then we can begin to process the papers."

"I have sent in several forms in the past. Isn't there any record of them on file?"

The clerk turned away to take a sip of coffee before replying. "I can't take the time to look for your file now, but nothing can be done until these new papers are filled out anyway."

"Do you think it will be possible for me to bring my wife into the US in a week?"

The clerk put her cup down and chuckled at my obvious ignorance. "No, after you fill out these forms they will be processed, that will take several weeks. Then, if everything is in order, your wife will be called for an interview, after which a visa can be issued. However, the first step is to fill these out," she said, pushing the remains of dead trees at me.

I knew my allotted time was over when the next number was called. Looking up at the Marine, I grabbed my papers with one hand, Iris with the other, turned, and left. That night was spent filling out the multitude of papers. Iris sat next to me as I tried to get the necessary information from her about her parents, her birthplace, and whatever else was needed to complete the application. Iris couldn't spell in English, and I couldn't spell in Hebrew, so we made up a new language of a bastard Hebrew-English, of which these forms were the first example.

A few days later we were back at the Embassy again in the endless line, again on the long wooden benches, again waiting, waiting, waiting. The couple next to us alternated naps so as not to miss hearing their number called over the loudspeaker. No one wanted to miss the call to the iron grating.

"Iris, maybe we should get married here at the embassy and live here. We could have babies and raise them here," I said, exasperated.

Finally, after some hours, our number was called. The clerk looked over our forms. I felt a new revelation in God as she declared the forms in order and asked for the seven-dollar application fee. I handed her an American ten-dollar bill.

"Oh, I am sorry, but this has to be in exact currency," she declared, with what I perceived was a gleeful smile over placing one more land mine in our way.

"Look, I don't have seven dollars. You can take the ten and keep the change, I really don't care. I just want to get out of here today," I said angrily.

The clerk waved me off. "Sorry, but that is against policy. When you get the exact change, you can come back." She looked past us to call the next number.

I turned to Iris to complain. "What the hell, I can't believe it. How am I going to get change of a ten without leaving the building and going to the bank? In the American embassy they don't even have change of a ten-dollar bill. What kind of stupid thing is this?"

We went down the rows of sleeping, half-sleeping, and semi-dead applicants, asking each one if they had change for a ten-dollar bill. It seemed a miracle when we found someone who had brought not only change but also a blanket, lunch, and dinner to the embassy. Armed with the seven exact American dollars, we charged back to the window.

"Here, here is the seven dollars," I triumphantly proclaimed.

The clerk looked up at us. Her completely bewildered expression reminded me of my college advisor when I informed him, I had gotten into medical school. Taking the currency, she admitted defeat as she wished us good luck in our marriage, told us not to expect to hear from the embassy for several weeks, and called out the next number.

I grabbed Iris and hugged and kissed her until the person behind me tapped me on the back to get out of the way so he could step to the window. We ran out of the embassy and down the street. We had done it! The Rabbinate, the embassy, the uncertainty of not knowing whether we could complete all the necessary preparations for our marriage were over. The only thing left was the marriage ceremony and for Iris to give notice to the army and await her visa.

That evening we went to the old city of Jaffa. Jaffa is a mostly Arab city built into the cliffs that rise above the Mediterranean Sea. Large rectangular blocks of stone make up the construction of the two- and three-story buildings with their arched entryways. Interspersed are the minarets, calling the Arab faithful to prayer. It was and still is a port city. Along the beachfront are cafés, and this is where Iris and I celebrated. As the sun shone off the waters of the Mediterranean, accenting a view that thousands if not millions have admired, we raised our glasses of wine and dreamed of what our new future would hold.

When we left the café, Iris kissed me with every step. By the time the evening came to an end, the skin was beginning to peel from my face from all the kissing.

We arrived home late that night to the consternation of Iris's parents, who reminded us that the one formality still left was our wedding, scheduled to take place in two days.

CHAPTER TWENTY-FIVE
The Wedding

Weddings have a universal nature. Everyone is insecure, no one is ready, the main participants are in doubt, the colors and clothes are wrong, and yet, despite all the difficulties, the marriage takes place. Ziggy was so calm it was as if he was marrying off someone else's daughter. He went about his duties like a proficient general. Noah was taken to the babysitter, Sarah and Iris to the beauty parlor. We checked on the hotel where we were to hold the ceremony to be sure it was ready.

When all that was completed, Ziggy had time to take me for a sightseeing tour of Jaffa and Tel Aviv. He explained various sights, checking his watch every half hour to be sure he was on time. I looked at my watch every fifteen minutes to be sure his watch was sure.

No wedding is complete without a last-minute emergency. When we arrived at the flower shop to pick up Iris's bouquet, it was not finished. But after some shouting and yelling, Ziggy obtained the flowers, and we headed back to the house. Ziggy was in control as he told me exactly how many minutes I had to change and get ready for the wedding. We both dressed, me in a white suit, Ziggy in a grey one. Sarah was already at the hotel with Iris. Ziggy patted me on the back, telling me not to be nervous as we entered the car and drove to the hotel for the wedding. We didn't talk much on the drive, Ziggy just saying, as best he could in English, that everything would go smoothly.

* * *

At the appointed hour everything was ready, and the wedding began.

I was sitting beside the rabbi, Ziggy, and Iris's grandfather Abraham, looking over the marriage contract. The rabbi, in English, explained some of the symbols and wording of the document. I looked it up and down, carefully reviewing it as best I could, not being able to read Hebrew.

He concluded by saying, "Now, I've explained to you what this contract means. It is customary in the Jewish religion to promise some amount of money to the wife in case the couple is divorced. How about two hundred thousand shekels?"

"Two hundred thousand shekels?" I whispered.

The rabbi, understanding that he had hit upon a note of discord, was quick to continue his explanation. "Now, you understand this is only ceremonial. Don't you think your wife is worth two hundred thousand shekels?" he said peering into my line of sight.

I thought to myself that not only was he a rabbi but a psychiatrist as well. With all the smiling faces looking at me I knew there was no negotiation, and I signed the contract. I joined the rest of the guests and family in the ballroom while thinking how much 200,000 shekels was in American dollars. As everyone was speaking Hebrew, I was left to think and talk to myself. I only knew one word in Hebrew— *shalom*—and was soon running out of variations of the pronunciation as I greeted each guest. There was a mixed crowd of people, some in suits, young adults in jeans, army officers in uniform and a few people who were either Iris's friends or had just walked in off the street.

The wedding was to be held in a small convention room. Being the sole member of my family present at the wedding, I looked for someone I recognized. Fortunately, I spotted Lillie, who had arrived from New York.

"Lillie, I'm glad to see you," I said as I kissed her on the cheek.

Lillie smiled. "Do you think I would miss my niece getting married? You look so nice."

"Have you seen Iris? She did come, didn't she?" I joked.

Lillie kept smiling. "Why, of course, do you think she's changed her mind? You know you are not supposed to see the bride before the wedding. However, Israeli marriages are not so strict; she should be out in a moment. I just saw her finish dressing. Relax, enjoy yourself, get to know the people. When you see her, it will be worth the wait. She is beautiful. You know I never realized my niece is so gorgeous."

Even on my wedding day I was sarcastic. "Lillie, I know she's beautiful, I knew it the first time I saw her. Do you think I've got bad taste? Now if she can cook, that will be great."

"Even if she can't cook, it will be okay. You take my word for it. Just be patient with her," Lillie said, grasping my arm. "Now turn around and take a look at your beautiful bride."

Iris was dressed in a white gown rimmed in gold lace that ended at her ankles. It was very simple, straight, no bows or train. On her head was a crown of flowers, a white carnation in her hair, and a veil covering it all. If she had makeup on, it was minimal. She just looked so innocent and very, very, beautiful. She had a half smile that looked to expand like the imminent breaking of a wave. She seemed to glide along as she walked. I was very proud.

Lillie, still next to me and still holding my arm, said the obvious. "You see, I tell you she's beautiful."

Iris walked up to some of her friends to greet them. She took a quick glance over her shoulder to make sure I was in the room, broke open her smile, and nodded to me. We were soon under the chuppah (a ceremonial fabric canopy held up by four poles that represents the home the couple will have together) before the rabbi and cantor. I stared at the rabbi, hoping he would keep his promise to guide me through the ceremony. I didn't want to marry the cantor by mistake. The ceremony proceeded well, I thought, as no one was leaving or laughing. The rabbi asked me to repeat after him a few words in Hebrew, then I slipped the wedding ring Iris had picked out on her finger. The veil was lifted as we both sipped wine from a cup. Iris shook her head tasting the wine; I think she preferred Coca-Cola. A few more words and singing in Hebrew. A glass was then placed beneath my foot for me to break (this represents that marriage involves sorrow and joy and dedication to your mate in bad as well as good times), and we were married. I moved my hands behind her head and directed her lips to mine, then held my bride very close. When we separated, I saw the corners of her mouth turn up in an ever-widening smile. She leaned against me as if her feet would not support her. All the insecurities about my intentions were now relieved, and her nervous anxiety gave way to exhaustion.

The celebration was not fancy, with about fifty guests present. The food was presented as a buffet—no tables. The music was recorded. It was very simple and intimate; it reminded me of an informal birthday party.

Iris soon regained her composure and was back to herself, greeting friends and accepting mazel toves (congratulations in Hebrew). In the interim, I hummed to the recorded Israeli songs. The guests happily danced. No one was in tuxedos, and many were dressed as if they had just come from work. I wondered at the younger men, looking so carefree, knowing how most of them had probably seen combat in war. The older people may have been holocaust survivors, it being 1981 and only thirty-six years since World War II had ended. It made me feel a little inadequate, as the only wars I had faced were the battles over my exams. But the most distressing thing to me was Sarah, dressed in black and never smiling, occasionally looking down at the ground as if she was searching for something she'd lost.

It was about three hours later that Iris and I reunited, went back to a hotel room for the evening, and sat with a bottle of wine.

"Well, Mrs. Jaffee, do you think you can at least spell your new name in English?" I said.

"Bob, I practice for two years, of course I know how," Iris said, snuggling into my lap. "Tell me, tell me that you love me. All the time it seem I force you to tell me that you love me."

"Of course I love you," I said, putting my arms around her waist.

"How much, how much?" she demanded.

I extended my arms to their full length. "This much, this much, and much, much more." I started to pull the zipper of her dress down. The dress released from its support fell to her ankles. I was stunned that her legs were covered in a haphazard railway of varicose veins.

"What happened to your legs? I never noticed that you had this problem." The words just burst out.

She told me that this was a new problem made worse by marching and standing in the army. "I hope it not bother you."

It did concern me. I wanted my wife to be perfect, but this wasn't her fault. "No, it doesn't bother me. It just seems unusual for such a young girl to have this problem. I think it should be checked into to see if there is anything wrong."

"We see, maybe when we get to States, we see." She then turned off the lights. In the dark the moon reflected off Iris as she finished undressing. Tall and slim, her contours seemed perfect. We were soon in bed.

"Bob, I love you," she whispered into my ear as she kissed me around the neck. "Bob, I want you."

I held her head with both my hands, bringing her mouth to mine. Once our lips were glued together, I released my hands to explore the rest of her. I reached around her buttocks, so round, so smooth. My hands traveled Like tourists in a foreign land, seeking new places to enjoy. Slipping down to her thighs, they headed to her vagina. I stopped to relax my lips and to gasp for more air to feed my racing system. Iris answered in echoing response to my deep breaths. I kissed her neck and advanced to her ear, sucking it and licking its crevices.

When I touched her clitoris, I could feel her momentarily stiffen as the delightful feeling spread through her. She gasped, taking her hands down to my penis to gently stroke it, back and forth, back and forth, letting it grow in her hands. I held her for support, expressing my satisfaction not only with soft groans but with increasing the force of my fingers on her back. I pushed my fingers into her vagina, so tight I wondered how my penis would ever fit. She moved about to find the best position for my hand then gently moved her hips in and out signaling her excitement by the intermittent stiffing of her body and heaving of her chest. When her body straightened up without relaxing, the sweat beading on her forehead, I knew she was reaching her climax. My hand pumped hard and fast in her vagina to give her the maximum feeling.

"Oh, Bob, so good, so good," she said, relaxing and rolling off me. Her head found itself beside my chest. She stroked it, kissing her way down to my penis. To be sure she didn't get lost, I guided her head to it. Slowly, so slowly her tongue wrapped itself around it, like tying a ribbon on a package. Then in one continuous gulp her mouth devoured it, releasing it again and again, until with a sudden, uncontrollable eruption I jammed her head as far down as her mouth would allow, tensed my muscles, and climaxed.

I lay nude on the bed, outstretched and exhausted. Good sex feels like the accomplishment of hard labor. It gives one the satisfaction of a job well done. I opened my eyes and looked around. The ecstasy was over, and it was to time to enter back to the real world. Although we had had sex before, this night seemed particularly satisfying.

"Where the hell did you learn to make love like that? I know you didn't learn it from me."

Iris had the devil's twinkle in her eyes. "Well, I not spend all my time in army learning how to fight. What you want? I wait for you all the time and not even sure if you come. You think I crazy?"

I sat up in bed and quizzed her. "Now tell me, you didn't get this from a book. This knowledge comes from experience. Who were you going to bed with?"

"It none of your business. Before we married you go to bed, you tell me, with lots of women why I not able to go to bed with men? You think you better than me? You think I go to bed with you because you know so much?"

"Men are supposed to know what to do," I said.

"Well how woman know if man do it right unless she also know what to do?"

I smiled to myself. Iris was hard to argue with and win. She was also avoiding answering my original question. "Look, I don't need a lesson in philosophy, I just want to know how you learned to make love. You do a good job of it. I'm not accusing you; after all, I told you in my letters to get some experience and go out with other men. I just want to find out how you learned."

Iris moved closer to me in bed and whispered in my ear, "Well, I live with camp commander."

"What? You lived with who and when?" I shouted.

"I thought you no get excited," she said quietly.

I regained my composure. "It's not excitement, just surprise. When were you living with him?"

"I live with him until week before you come to Israel."

Again, I raised my voice. "What, you mean you were living with him when I was calling you up each week? How did you manage that? What the hell was going on?"

"Why you get excited? You tell me to go out with men," she said with a smile.

I tried to be more placid. "No, no, I'm not excited, but just how were you able to manage that?"

"Well, it not easy to go home every Saturday to get your call but I manage. He very nice man. We have good time together and he teach me many things."

I realized what he had been teaching her. "How did you know that you weren't going to marry him?"

Iris laughed like the answer was obvious. "Oh, I sure I not marry him. I not love him. He playboy."

I scratched my head. "You mean to tell me you lived with him but were sure you didn't love him?"

To Iris the answer was simple: "Yes, that's right. I love you," she said leaning over to kiss me. "Bob, you think you ever cheat on me? Now tell me the truth," she implored. "No joke with me."

I placed my hand beneath my chin for support, thinking what a loaded question this was. "Hmm, no, I don't think so. I think if you love somebody, then you don't cheat on them. It's not that I never want to go to bed with another woman, I mean I'm sexually attracted to other women, but it just wouldn't be fair to the one you love." I hoped I was telling the truth. "And what about you? How do you know you wouldn't cheat on me?"

Iris answered without hesitation. "I don't know. It silly to say what will happen in future. How I able to tell you that I no cheat? It may come that I meet very handsome man and that I go to bed with him. It silly to sit here and say things never to change that what today we feel and say we always be. I hope we be together forever, be happy, have lots of children, but who knows what happen?"

I smiled to myself. It was not the answer I expected. Who could tell the future? Oh well, the hell with philosophy. We went back to making love.

The next morning I awoke before Iris. Again, I wondered how Iris would adapt to the United States and especially to Texas. We had been together less than three months in the previous two years, three months between two people separated by language, culture, age, education, seemingly everything that made people compatible. How could one say this was the basis for a happy marriage?

When Iris awoke, we went back to gathering the necessary papers for her visa. There was no time for a honeymoon. Then it was to her parents' house for me to pack. Soon we were back at the airport again saying goodbye. This time Iris could at least stare at her new ring with satisfaction.

"I come as soon as I can. Now you see about school for me so I able to do something in States. And Bob, I love you very much, I think about you every day and will call you," she said as we embraced.

I guess romance was not my forte. "I love you very much, but if you call me every day, we will soon be broke. I'll call you once a week to see how things are progressing. Okay?"

"Oh, you no love me. You always concerned with money," Iris replied with a huff.

As the call to board was announced, I said my goodbyes. "Remember I love you and I want you to come as soon as possible." A hug, a squeeze, a kiss, and I was on the plane to return to the States.

It was now Dr. and Mrs. Jaffee. On the return flight I thought of the consequences of my marriage. I was taking a young woman away from all that was familiar to her to live with me in Texas. Add to this the stress of being a wife, and me a husband. Neither of us had any practical experience in the matter.

Is this going to work?

CHAPTER TWENTY-SIX
Back to Texas

The next few weeks passed as I waited anxiously for Iris to finish her visa application. After three weeks she had conquered the last obstacle and had the visa as well as the airline tickets for the United States. I felt like I was age seven, waiting weeks and weeks for some cereal giveaway, and finally, finally receiving the prize.

There was now nothing left in the way of preliminary preparations for Iris's arrival. It had been almost two years since I had met Iris in Monticello and a month since our marriage in Israel.

* * *

My heart raced excitedly as, arriving at the airport, I looked expectantly for my nineteen-year-old bride. Where could she be? Passenger after passenger came off with no sign of Iris.

Could she have taken the wrong flight?

I stood on my toes, straining to see. I was thinking I might have to rescue her from some foreign land when I caught a glimpse of a woman's head with long blond hair bobbing up and down. When the people in front of her had cleared, I could see, finally, Mrs. Jaffee. Haltingly at first then picking up the pace to a gallop she came toward me. Before I could blurt out a single word I was engulfed in hugs and kisses.

After we kissed a hundred times, I was able to welcome her and ask her about the trip.

"Oh, it a little difficult for me, but I do it. I so happy to see you that I not able to remember nothing else," Iris said as she wrapped herself around me.

The sun was just setting as we drove home. I tried to point out the sites as we passed the oil refinery, the oil rigs, the heavy machinery shops, and the vast flatness of land that seemed to creep forward endlessly. Iris looked from side to side—not that the view was much different on the right as opposed to the left.

"Isn't the sunset beautiful? They say the sunsets here are the most beautiful in the country. I tell everyone it's because there is nothing to obstruct the view, nothing else to look at," I said.

"Bob, they have tree here?" she said with a puzzled look.

I smiled. "They have some nice plastic trees, but the only real ones are in a museum."

We went out for dinner to celebrate. As I had done in the past, I ordered for the both of us. Even with so much to discuss, because of her fatigue from her long flight, we ate in silence and then returned to my apartment.

A faint smile came over Iris as she viewed the Welcome banner I had placed. It was 10PM and being tired Iris did not unpack but brushed her teeth and slipped on a nightgown as she climbed into bed.

As we turned the lights off to go to sleep, Iris turned to me. "You love me?"

No matter how many times I had told her she seemed always in doubt. "Of course, I love you very much," I replied.

"Bob, hold me."

I put my arms around her and held her for a few minutes. "Iris, it's hard for me to sleep like this. I have to turn to the other side to get comfortable," I said as I released my hold and turned away. I could hear soft crying. I turned back again and put my arms around her. I didn't ask what was wrong. She was only nineteen, away from home, without friends, coping with the shock of a foreign culture and language. I just waited until she fell asleep. There would be a lot of adjustments for Iris to find happiness with me in this place.

It's up to me to smooth the path. I must not fail her.

CHAPTER TWENTY-SEVEN
The First Week

*T*he next morning, I woke before Iris and looked at my new wife. *How strange to have somebody next to me.*

I covered Iris up with the blanket and quietly got dressed. As I was sneaking out the door to go to work, I heard a yell from the bedroom.

"Stop, wait!" Iris commanded.

I halted. "What's wrong? I'm just going to work. I didn't want to wake you."

"What you forget you married already? You no kiss me when you leave?" Iris shouted.

I returned to the bedroom. Iris was sitting up in bed, arms folded across her chest, a frown on her face. I kissed her on the forehead as she grabbed me around my head and planted a second kiss to my lips.

Untangling myself from her grip, I announced that I would be home for lunch and left for work.

* * *

Arriving back for lunch, I found Iris just awakening.

"Well, where is lunch? I thought it was the wife's job to make lunch for her husband," I said jokingly, looking at the empty dining-room table.

"Now, first thing you do is give me kiss. Before you complain you kiss me, and you no forget that," she said pointing a finger at me.

I gave Iris a quick kiss to the cheek.

"What, you call that a kiss?" she complained.

I repeated the kiss until it could pass muster. However, that still didn't solve the question of lunch.

I went into the kitchen and pulled from the freezer a frozen pizza, placing it in the microwave. Iris came out of the bedroom and placed herself at the dining table to await being served. When the buzzer sounded, I cut the pizza into slices and divided it on two plates placing her lunch in front of her.

Iris sat in her red bathrobe taking small bites of her slice.

"Ich!" she said, throwing the bitten pizza down on the plate. "This awful. How you eat this?" She marched to the kitchen and pulled out some bread, cheese, and vegetables and proceeded to make herself lunch.

"What I do this afternoon?" she said.

I swallowed a bite of pizza, which did have a great similarity to cardboard. "Well, why don't you go to the shopping center across the street? It will give you something to do. I think the first thing we must do is to get you a driver's license and a job. I will also investigate the local college. You must do something, so you don't just sit here all day."

Iris frowned, pounding her fists into her lap. "Bob, you find me a job?"

"I can't find you a job. You go across the street and see if you can find yourself a job." I got up to wash my hands. Iris trailed behind.

"No one want me. I no talk well and no understand the money here. Who going to hire me?"

"If you don't look, you will not find. At least look, make some effort. I will help you with the things you may have to know to work. You need to build up your confidence, and that can only happen if you start to do things without me. I know it's difficult but start. Go into the stores and ask for a job. The worst they can say is no." I dried my hands, leaned over and gave her a kiss. She put her arms to her sides and stood slumped over, looking at the ground as I started to leave.

"You call me, don't forget to call me," she begged.

It was a busy day at work. It wasn't until three in the afternoon that I remembered to call home. The phone rang five, six, seven times before a distant-sounding voice answered.

"Yes, I sleeping. When you be home?" Iris said.

I told her how busy the office was, and I was not sure exactly when I would return. "Did you go to the shopping center?" I asked.

"No, I not want to go alone," she said softly.

I could sense Iris's loneliness, and it hurt me to feel her distress. "Maybe when I get back from work, we will go together."

"Bob, you be home soon. Okay?" she implored. "Bob, I love you."

When I arrived home, I found Iris still in bed. I leaned over her. She turned toward me as she said, "Give me a kiss."

"I'll give you a kiss if you get up and give me dinner."

She took a deep breath and expelled it forcibly. "Forget it, forget it, go away."

"What do you mean? First you want a kiss and now you don't. What's with you?"

"No, no, no. You want somebody to make you dinner. You not want wife. You get yourself dinner, forget you married," she said, turning to wrap herself in the bed covers.

I didn't think this would create such a stir. But with the shock of coming to the States, I could understand her frustration. "Now, of course I want a wife, that's why I married you. But I also like to eat," I said.

Iris just slipped further under the bedcovers. I jumped into bed after her and started to tickle her, then held her as she again asked if I was sure I wanted her as a wife.

"I'm sure, very sure. Now, get out of bed. It's almost time to go back to sleep for the evening, at least get up for a little while." After a couple more minutes of hugging, she got up without reply and dressed. As she dressed, I went into the kitchen to look for something to eat. Finding some chicken, I started to cook, beckoning Iris to come over, watch, and learn. She came in, looked over my shoulder with a blank expression, turned, went to the living room, and sat down on the couch.

"Now what is wrong? Come here and learn something."

Iris didn't move. "I no need to watch you to learn how to cook. I not going to learn by watching you. I will learn on my own." She put her feet up on the couch and turned her back to me.

It was not possible to move this woman sitting on the couch like some entrenched bridge pillar.

I finished making dinner. Iris came to the table to pick at the food. I grew increasingly frustrated and I again asked her what the problem was.

Iris shrugged. "What I do tomorrow?" she said, looking down at her plate.

"I don't know. Perhaps try to go to the mall and look for a job," I said. She didn't answer but just shrugged a second time.

"Perhaps you can go out with some of the people at my office. They are a little older than you, but you're just as mature, and maybe you will find a friend."

There was no reply as she got up, went back to the bedroom, and fell back asleep.

* * *

A few days passed. At the clinic people were interested in finding out about Iris, this woman from a foreign land. "What is she like? How is she adjusting? What is she doing?"

I felt a faint smile tickle my lips. "Well, it's quite a new experience to be cursed at in Hebrew. As soon as we speak the same language, we can communicate, and I'll be able to answer your questions." I didn't want to tell them the truth, so making a joke sufficed.

"We all want to meet her. How about we have a welcome party for her next Friday? We can use the clinic. About five o'clock?" asked Libby.

I was happy to accept. It would give everyone the opportunity to meet and talk to Iris, and maybe she would make friends.

When I arrived home that evening, Iris was asleep again. I looked at her, all curled up in bed. Her face seemed to have gullies from the continuous steam of tears. She was awakened by my presence and opening her eyes, reached out her arms, beckoning me to get in the bed. We hugged, and surprisingly, she announced that she was going to prepare dinner.

"Tonight, I make you shakshuka. I know you will like it; we eat it all the time in Israel," she proudly said.

It sounded like nothing I had ever heard of before. I thought it might be some nice lamb or spicey Mediterranean dish. Iris got out of bed, dressed and went into the kitchen to start preparing dinner while I went to the living room to wait.

I got up from the couch, where I had been relaxing, went to the kitchen and peered over her shoulder. In the frying pan were tomatoes, green peppers, eggs, and various spices. I wasn't sure if it was soup or food for people without teeth. I kept my thoughts to myself as I sat back down. Iris placed the shakshuka on a plate and took out a can of corn, opened the lid and placed it on the table.

I was stunned. "What is this cold corn on the table for?"

"We are going to have corn also. Now give me your plate and I give you some shakshuka."

The shakshuka seemed lubricated enough to slide down your throat before you could taste it. The cold corn in the can made me feel I was marooned on some island.

I looked up at Iris, laughing. "Maybe in your country you don't take the corn out of the can and heat it, but in the US we do."

She put her fork down. "I don't understand what bad. In Israel we eat cold corn. This is the way I used to. You no have to laugh about it, it not funny."

"I'm sorry for laughing. It is just that I'm not used to eating this type of food. I'll have to show you how to make things we eat in the US, meat and potatoes, chicken, and things like that."

"You don't like this?" Iris said, staring me in the eye. "You no have to lie to me. If you no like it you can tell me."

"Well, it's just different. It's not that I don't like it. It's just that I'm not used to it." I said, trying to extricate myself from the conversation without hurting her feelings.

Iris turned away and looked down at the food. "I sorry, this all I know how to make. I sorry you no like it, but I try, and there nothing wrong with it."

I got up and put my arm around Iris, kissing her on her wet cheek. She pushed me aside as she got up and cleared the table.

After she washed the dishes and cleaned up the kitchen, she went into the bedroom and closed the door. I sat at the dining table with my head in my hands, asking myself why I had been so inconsiderate.

I went to the bedroom knowing I would find Iris crying. She was sitting at the edge of the bed wiping copious tears that streamed down her face. I sat down next to her and gently placed her head in my lap.

"I know you put a lot of work into dinner. I am just not used to that kind of food. It will take me time, but it was very good, really."

She sat up, wiping away some tears. "You lie, you lie. You no like it. I think nothing I do here you like."

I raised my voice. "Now stop it, that is not true. Don't make so much out of this. You'll learn to cook more things."

"No, no, it not only that you not like it. You make fun of it."

I tried to retract my earlier comments. "I'm not making fun of it. I'm sorry if it sounded like that, but I'm not. It's just that it struck me a little funny because I'm not used to eating cold corn or shakshuka, but I'm not making fun of you."

The argument was escalating. "Yes, you are," she said softly. "I don't think I fit in here."

"You will. Give yourself some time. You've only been here a short time, give yourself time. You can always go back to Israel, but a few days is not really a fair trial. Give yourself some time," I said.

I held Iris while she cried herself to sleep.

What an awful beginning.

CHAPTER TWENTY-EIGHT
The Party

O n Friday afternoon we went to the clinic welcoming party. I hoped it would make her feel more comfortable in this foreign land.

"Now, Iris, I told you about the people in the clinic. Hopefully, you will meet someone to be friends with. I want you to start establishing some sort of life on your own. Okay?" I said to her as she shrugged and turned to look out the car window.

When we arrived at the clinic, she just walked in with her head down. All the people from the clinic and some of my friends came forward to introduce themselves to her. Iris picked up her head and a smile came across her face as she put out her hand to each one, saying hello in her thick accent. We assembled in the large clinic waiting room.

Iris was led to a wicker chair that looked like something for a Polynesian princess. She took a seat as the clinic's employees presented her with small gifts, dishtowels, cooking utensils or glassware. A smile and a thank you were given in return.

A cake was cut in the middle of the waiting room and we milled around, making conversation between bites.

Ellen, one of the clinic secretaries, came up to Iris. "How do you like Odessa?"

Iris smiled politely. "It very new to me. It very nice."

Libby, one of the ophthalmic techs, presented herself to make an offer. "I'm so glad to meet you. Dr. Jaffee has talked a lot about you. Sometime you must come with us when we go out or go bowling."

Iris responded without much energy: "Yes, yes I think that be nice."

We bumped into Curtis, who as usual was at no loss for words. "Well, you must be Iris. Bob told me you were beautiful, but I wasn't prepared for such a lovely woman. I'm very pleased to make your acquaintance," he boomed, extending his hand.

If Iris couldn't talk to Curtis, who could carry on a monologue from birth to death in an empty room, she couldn't talk to anyone. "Curtis is probably the most genuine Texan I've ever met," I commented. "If you're looking for the entire culture of Texas, he's it. He looks like a Texan, dresses like one, and talks like one."

Curtis was never shy. "Hell, man! If you want to know what it's like to be in Texas, you just ask me. I can tell you where to get the best boots, the best hats, and the best chicken-fried steak around. I know where to get the best rattlesnake belt buckles."

I laughed. "I don't think a rattlesnake buckle is what she needs right now. But she does need a hairdresser. I told her you're the best in Texas."

Curtis's mustache curled upwards. "Hon, anything you need in the way of hair care I can give. You just come over to my shop and we'll fix you up so good Bob will not even recognize you."

"Curtis, she's beautiful now," I said.

"Hell, man I know that, and I aim to keep her that way," Curtis said stretching out his arms for added emphasis.

Iris was laughing, watching Curtis and I fight over her. She turned to Curtis. "You think you can take care of me? "

"Hell, no problem. It's my job, and if there is one thing I know, it's how to cut hair. Why don't you come next week, and I'll cut and set it for you? It will give us a chance to talk, and I can tell you all about Odessa. Why, you'll feel like a native after I get done with you. There is one thing you and Bob must do and that is come to dinner with me and Diane. I know you will like Diane, you and she will get along great, like two rabbits in mating season."

I thought, why wait? and suggested we go out that evening. Curtis called Diane and she agreed to meet us. Since Iris had never eaten Mexican cuisine, we decided that would be our choice. Charles, my internist friend, and his wife, Mary, not having had a chance to talk to Iris at the party, also wanted to come. The three cars followed one another to the restaurant.

We arrived at the restaurant, El Mexican, and were shown to a table. The restaurant had several Mexicans speaking Spanish and eating which gave a feeling of authenticity to the place. The wooden tables weren't much but the walls were gaily painted with scenes of Mexican dancers with large sombreros. Iris was perplexed by the menu; English was difficult enough, and she had not a prayer to comprehend Spanish. I went through the menu and made suggestions.

Mary, sitting on the other side of my wife, drawled, "Oh, Iris, you're so precious. You're just what I expected, from Bob's description. I hope we will have lots of chances to get together. I can take you shopping and show you the stores in the area."

Charles chuckled and winked. "Yes, I can assure you Mary is very good in knowing where to spend money."

Iris gave Mary a half-hearted smile. "Yes, I think I would enjoy that."

"How are you adjusting to the English language?" Diane asked.

"It very difficult. It take time for me to learn."

Curtis had to add his opinion. "Now look, any country that has the best army in the world can learn a little English. I'm sure Iris will learn to speak it so well her mother won't even recognize her voice."

I wanted to show off my "warrior." "Iris was in the army, you know. She even got to ride in a tank. I don't know what the war effort gained from this, but she said it was a lot of fun."

Iris frowned. "Yes, I get to ride tank, but only one time. I not trained in riding tank."

"Well, you see, you see, even their women ride tanks. Hell, when I was in Vietnam, I must have been in three or four types of tanks. I knew how to ride almost all the tanks the US had, even the very latest ones," Curtis said, waving his hand for emphasis.

Mary put her hand on Iris's shoulder. "My, how precious, imagine a little darling like you in a tank. You must have been scared."

Charles added sarcastically, "I don't know, I think it's a good idea for women to be in tanks; that way they'd be a lot quieter."

Iris just sat attentively looking at each speaker but adding little to the conversation. The rest of us babbled our way through dinner. Iris made appointments to meet Mary the following week and to have Curtis do her hair.

When we got into the car and were alone, I immediately wanted to know if Iris felt she had made any friends. She shrugged. It was getting so that I could sense her shrugging without even watching.

"I no think so," she said. "Mary much different than me. I don't think I have anything to say to her. She no understand anything about me or my country. They think it joke I in army."

When I asked about Diane and Curtis, there was a glimmer of hope: "I think I like Diane and Curtis, but I feel they older than me. Diane very nice, she quiet but nice. Curtis, he very funny. I like him."

"Well, at least that's something. I was afraid you would hate everyone," I said.

* * *

As we were about to go to sleep, Iris tapped me on the shoulder.

"Bob, I no able to go to sleep unless you hold me. Bob, hold me. You love me?" she asked.

I turned toward Iris and held her. I again told her how much I loved her. Sleep was not to come until the soft accompaniment of her crying had subsided.

Progress? Not much.

CHAPTER TWENTY-NINE
Problems, Problems, Problems

The next morning Iris got up early and first thing called her parents. They spoke in Hebrew as I just stood there, calculating the cost per minute of the call. After a while I could not contain myself. "Iris, you've been on the phone for twenty minutes. Life can't be that bad. You can call again next week. Get off the phone."

Iris turned around and yelled, "*Sheket!*" ("quiet" in Hebrew). Then realizing she would do better in English, she said, "Bob, leave me alone. I can't hear with you talking."

I walked out of the room shaking my head, not able to understand what mistreatment she had suffered that caused her to talk for so long. I was blind to how lonely this woman was and her need for family support. I went into the living room to count the minutes and dollars until Iris was finished.

Finally, after thirty minutes, she was done. I called her into the living room, hardly able to contain my anger. "Thirty minutes on the phone. Do you realize how much that costs? Couldn't you write them a letter? That call cost one hundred dollars."

Iris just shrugged, sat down, and began to read one of her Hebrew books.

"Stop reading when I'm talking to you. I think maybe since you're going to spend so much time on the phone, you should call every second or third week. At a hundred dollars a week we can't afford these calls," I said, raging on.

"No, Bob, this I no discuss with you," she said, getting up and heading for the bedroom.

Fortunately I was on emergency call, and at that moment the phone rang. I was summoned to the hospital. I left Iris without a word and didn't return until four hours later, when I was finished with the emergency.

Iris was curled up on the sofa next to her book, sleeping. I took the opportunity to call Steven in New York to vent some of my discontent.

When Steven answered, he immediately got to the point. "How is the newly married man making out?"

"Well, I don't know."

"What's the matter? You don't sound too enthusiastic about it," Steven said.

"Well, I just don't know. There are so many problems, I just don't know if we can work them all out. She can't cook, she doesn't clean the house, she doesn't do the laundry, she can't drive a car, she doesn't have a job and she feels miserable."

"Bob, these are small things. She will learn to cook and drive. She'll get a job. Relax. Give her time to adjust. It's not easy. Think what it would be like if you were in Israel. You must bear with her for a while."

"I hope we will stay together long enough for us to get everything straightened out. This morning she was on the phone for half an hour talking to her mother. A half hour at three dollars a minute."

"You will have to explain this to her. Don't judge everything based on a few weeks. Now perk up. You know you can always talk to me if you have any problems. But don't be in such a hurry to give up. Remember how much this girl gave up to marry a slob like you. Now, it's up to you to help make it work."

I took a deep breath. "Yeah, I guess you're right. It's kind of silly to expect so much after a couple of weeks. Oh well, okay. I'll speak to you in a week or two and let you know how things are progressing."

After the conversation I felt more conciliatory towards Iris. I went into the living room, put my arms around her and gave her a kiss. She awoke and put her arms around me and hugged me as if nothing had happened— there was no animosity from our morning argument.

It was still early in the afternoon, so I suggested we go to the mall across the street and search for a job for her. We found a store that was offering employment.

"I no want to go in alone. You come with me," Iris said, pulling me along.

"No, it looks better if you go in by yourself. Don't worry, the worst they can say is no. But you must get started. There is nothing that is going to make it any easier. Just go in and ask for an application." I gave her a kiss and sent her in. I sat and waited wondering if we both had taken on more than we could handle

Was it a mistake to marry Iris and bring her to the US? Could she adjust? Could I adjust?

* * *

It was May 1981, and Iris had been in the United States for six weeks.

That evening, I went to work preparing dinner, objecting: "Now, Iris, this has got to stop. You must learn to cook. I already have a job to support us and pay for your phone bills. Your job, while you sit here doing nothing all day, is to learn how to cook and take care of the house." I pointed at the untidy room and continued. "Look at it, it's a mess. You don't do anything all day. You must make some effort to contribute."

There was no verbal reply. She sat in the corner, looking at one of her books. She ate little that evening for dinner. After dinner I picked up the plates and put them in the sink, then sat down to catch up on my medical reading. Iris cleaned the dishes by hand and put them away. I was glad she had decided to do some work. As I had fallen behind in my medical reading, there were many journals awaiting my attention.

Iris cleaned up the kitchen and sat down to watch TV.

"Turn off the TV. I can't read with that thing on," I said.

"What you think I do here while you read? I have nothing to do." Iris got up, shut the TV off, and went into the bedroom, slamming the door.

I sat staring at the journal I'd been trying to read but thinking about what was happening. This marriage wasn't going well. Didn't she understand she was married to a physician? Reading medical journals, taking emergency calls, going to medical meetings in and out of town were all necessary parts of my life. My job wasn't nine to five.

But what of *her* needs? It must have been incredibly difficult for a nineteen-year-old to give up so much to come live here in the States with me. I was confused over what I owed my work versus what I owed my wife. I had never married, never been in this situation, and I was not able to appreciate what Iris was going through or how to help her.

Is she failing to be a wife or am I failing to be a husband?

* * *

The following day I dropped Iris off at the salon for her hair appointment with Curtis and continued to the clinic.

When I returned a couple of hours later, the richness in color and luster of her hair was matched by the buoyancy and vivaciousness of her personality. She was laughing and talking to the employees of the store.

"Wow, you look great!" I said admiringly.

"Well, hell man, of course she looks good. I told you I was going to make her look even more beautiful. We had a long talk. I even gave her the number of some Israeli customers of mine for her to call. Bob, you sure are one lucky, man. She's beautiful, and talking to her, I could tell she's one intelligent chick," Curtis said.

Iris just laughed and leaned her head on my shoulder.

On the way home she commented: "Curtis so funny. He keep me laughing. He tell me how you and him meet and about him and Diane and how he fight in war. He tell me about all the armies of the world. He invite us to have dinner with him and Diane. He also give me people from Israel to call up." She gasped for a breath. "Imagine, Bob, there're other people from Israel here. Also, Curtis do good job on hair. He say I need to come back every week."

She moved closer to me in the car and in a soothing voice asked, "How work go for you?"

If Iris was bubbly, I was not. "I'm unhappy seeing emergencies all day while other people get the surgical patients. Everyone wants to see Dr. Sheets. All I get are the patients he doesn't want. I want to do more surgery."

Iris's gaze was glued on me. "Bob, you very smart. One day you have big practice of your own. It just take time so people get to know you. But Dr. Sheets boss now, so you have to wait."

She was right, I was being impatient. I took a deep breath trying to accept I was the low man on the totem pole.

On the way back we made a stop at the grocery store. Iris and I went up and down the aisles, with me making the selections as Iris was not familiar with the brands and English labels.

"Do we need soap?" I asked. Iris just shrugged.

"Do we need paper towels?" Iris shrugged.

"Iris, do we need milk?" Again, a shrug.

"You're supposed to be doing something at home, at least looking at what we need. Now I don't want this to happen again. You're to take care of the house."

"Why I take care of house? You eat at house. You sleep at house. It not for me to do all the work. I will help, but I not only one to take care of house."

"What do you mean, we share work at the house? When you

share my work at the office, I'll share the work at the house." I moved on to gather the milk and butter.

Iris calmly replied, "Bob, this not way it going to be. I not going to stay home all day to take care of house and do cleaning. This not the way I am and that not the way I going to be."

I let it go without replying. With that, we finished shopping and went home.

How much longer can this marriage last?

I felt my obligation in a marriage was to provide an income and that Iris's duty was to cook and take care of the house. I was still stuck in the expectations of 1950s television shows. Iris wanted a life of her own as an equal partner in marriage, not a subservient role to me.

Is it me that needs to adjust, to understand, to mature? Maybe.

CHAPTER THIRTY
New Friend, Old Problems

The next week Iris told me of her plans to meet the Israelis that Curtis had mentioned. Obviously, she was excited about meeting someone from home.

"I wonder why people from Israel come here. Why I not understand. I think if I had choice I live in Israel. Bob, maybe someday we go live in Israel."

"You just got to the US, and you want to go back and live in Israel already? We will see, maybe, but I doubt it. They have lots of doctors in Israel and they don't need me. I don't think I could fit in there."

Iris was hopeful. "Well, we see. Maybe if you find job there you work there"

I gave Iris a kiss, wished her a good time, with her new acquaintances and went to work.

That evening, tired of cooking, we went out for dinner. Iris gave me a report on how her afternoon went with the new friends.

"Oh Bob, it very nice to speak Hebrew with someone. Her name Carmella and she very interesting. Her husband, Avi, went from Israel two years ago to Colombia and become fisherman. Now they in Texas for work. She seem very nice. She have child three years old and he very cute. We go and walk in shops and do a lot of talking." Iris said between bites. Her face was lit up with excitement. "Her husband build houses. She tell me about how she met husband, and about South America and here. I tell her about you and my family. Tomorrow, we go again. She not have job and she able to drive car, so she come over and get me."

I was glad Iris had found a person she could relate to. I hoped this would make her transition to this country easier.

As we got up to leave the restaurant, Iris whispered in my ear to kiss her.

"Here in the restaurant? I don't think it will look good."

She was adamant. "I no care how it looks. I want kiss."

I continued on toward the exit. As we approached the parking lot, I looked around to make sure no one was watching before I grabbed Iris and kissed her. I didn't want us to be a spectacle. I don't know why I was so self-conscious. I should have realized Iris was correct: Who cared?

* * *

It was important for Iris to learn how to drive. I went to the motor vehicle department and picked up a driving manual for her to study. When I arrived home that afternoon, Iris, as usual, was waiting. But instead of sleeping, she was up, vibrant, and smiling.

"I go out with Carmella again today and think maybe I get job. I go into store and speak to manager. He like me very much, tell me to fill out application and come back. It store that sell clothes. You help me fill out application tonight?'

I was happy to assist. "Of course, I'll help. But tell me more what you and Carmella talked about."

"We talk about the temple here. She tell me how funny she think it is. She say it much different than temple in Israel. It very simple and have a lot of English that we not have in Israel. In Israel it very serious—no joking or laughing, everything done in Hebrew. She say here it not serious. Maybe one time we go when they go so I able to see what it like. And Bob, I want that you meet them. They invite us over for dinner, so we go?"

I was glad Iris was making some acquaintances and readily agreed to take her to temple and have dinner with her new Israeli friends. Iris was in such a good mood that she offered to make dinner that evening, which surprised me. I didn't want to hurt her feelings by asking for something she couldn't make, so I suggested the one dish she could make: shakshuka.

"But I thought you not like shakshuka," Iris said raising her eyebrows.

"No, It's just different to me. I think I'd like to try it again." I could always find something to eat later, I thought.

Iris was delighted that she was called upon to make her favorite and only dish. The smell of paprika, onions and garlic permeated the air. I could hear the metal spoon mixing the ingredients in the pan while waiting in the living room. I was determined to give this dish a fair chance to impress me.

As we sat down to eat, the food seemed more palatable. I tried not to swallow it so fast that I might taste it before it slid into my stomach. I can't say it was enjoyable, but I felt after a few more times I would learn to tolerate it, maybe even like it. I was also glad she didn't put out the can of cold corn.

While eating, Iris asked about going to school.

"What do you want to study?"

"I not know, but I think it important that I go and learn something. When I in school then I find something that I like. I hope they let me in. I hope they no see that I fail math in school. I never able to pass math. I not do well in final exam, and they not pass me in it."

"You mean you flunked math in high school?" I said as my eyebrows went up in disbelief.

Iris waved her hand as if to push mathematics away from the table. "It not important. I just not able to do math. I take final exam but I not able to concentrate. I sit down and look at test then get up and leave."

"You mean you just got up and left without even taking it? Why didn't you try?" I said.

"Oh, Bob, why waste time? I look at exam and know I not able to do it, so why waste time and get same result? I go to beach and get tan."

I laughed. "You went to the beach instead of taking your exam! My mother is a schoolteacher. If she heard that, she would have forbidden our getting married."

Iris took this seriously. "It nothing to laugh about. I just have block in head. I just not able to do. I hope this not keep me out of school."

I was still laughing. "Well, we will go and see. Maybe if you bring your grades in Hebrew, they'll never know you flunked."

I had thought Iris was making real progress toward integrating with American society; that evening, however, she softly cried herself to sleep again.

On the next Saturday Iris was again on the phone to her parents. I objected, again, after she had spent forty minutes on the phone, and she, again, yelled *sheket*. When she had finished with her call, she came charging out of the bedroom.

"Bob, I no want you to bother me when I on the phone. This only chance I have to speak to family and I not able to speak with you yelling. Now you leave me alone."

It was hard to argue with someone who turned their back on you and walked away. I still only saw dollars and not her loneliness and the need for family support.

On Saturday afternoon, Iris went shopping with Mary. I spent the time reading and was home when Iris returned three hours later. I was hoping she had found another friend. When I asked about her feelings, she just shrugged and dropped down on the sofa.

"Bob, I right. I not think that she and I be good friends. She tell me all about she and husband how they have problems. I listen to her but not able to say anything back to her. How I able to tell her about husband? It not for me to tell her such thing. I don't know why people tell me their problems. I have not answer. But I listen."

The answer was obvious to me. "Well, that's it! That's why they tell you. You listen, which is probably more than they get from anybody else."

Iris let out a deep sigh. "I not know. I only know that I no want to talk to her again about her problems."

"Yes, you're right. Speaking of marriages, you have enough problems with your own marriage. Did you at least get a chance to tell her about your problems with me?"

Iris sat up straight. "Oh, of course not. It none of her business what bad between you and me. We keep problems here. It not good for her to tell me what she not like. Nothing I can do."

"Make her feel better. Make up something, tell her I hit you. Maybe in comparison her husband won't look so bad."

She looked directly at me. "This not something to joke on. If you ever touch me, I blow you up, and that something you can be sure of."

I should have changed the subject but mistakenly continued jesting. "Now, who is boss in this house? I am, right? And if I boss, can't I hit wife occasionally?"

There was not a hint of a smile on Iris's face as she told me. "There no boss in house. There two equal people—no boss."

"Well, I can see it's going to be tough to boss you around, especially if you shoot me dead. Anyway, speaking of sad things, how are you doing on your driving manual?"

"I not think I able to do it. I not understand the words."

"I'll help you. But you're the one who has to take the test. Put. more effort into It." I slowly emphasized each word.

"No, no. You yell and get upset. I not ever want you to yell at me."

She got up and walked to the kitchen. Following her, I found Iris crying. "I think there may be nothing for me to do except for me to leave," she blurted out.

I put my arm around her. I felt humbled. She looked so hurt. What could I do? I couldn't make friends for her; I couldn't take the driving test for her; I couldn't even speak her language. But I could be more sympathetic.

I told her that it would be okay, that I would help her with the driver's manual.

"It's not just that. It's everything. I never able to adjust. I never able to fit in here. I think it better that I not make you and me unhappy and go back to Israel," she said, wiping the tears from her face.

"This will all pass. You will succeed here; I know you will. I want you to. I don't want you to go back to Israel. Please don't give up." I said. I hid my head behind her shoulders so she wouldn't see my tears.

"No, no. It better I go back. It will never work. I just fool myself," she insisted.

I used my sleeve to wipe away my tears and looked at Iris. I had an idea. "I'll tell you what I'm going to do. I'm going to put money in a bank account for you to take out to go to Israel. I don't want you to feel you have to stay here if you don't want to. I don't want you to feel like a trapped animal. For this reason, the money will be under your name so you can take it out anytime you feel you must go back." I paused to kiss Iris on the cheek, soaking up some of the salty tears on her face. "But I do want you to know that I love you very much and hope that time will never come."

Iris stopped to wipe her face. "Why you want me here? I no good. I not able to do anything."

"I want you here because I want you as my wife. Because I love you. I know you are unhappy now, but you are young. You don't have to decide today, tomorrow, this week, or even this month. Just give yourself some time. That's all I ask."

We conversed back and forth as I tried to give Iris some confidence that she would make it, that she would overcome the difficulties of the cultural barrier and loneliness. I did not want to lose her.

She will make it here. She is strong, I know it. Just give her more time.

We reached no conclusion. She ended the conversation with her signature shrug.

CHAPTER THIRTY-ONE
Starting to Adjust

*I*t was June, and Iris had been in the United States for almost three months. My work at the clinic was progressing. I had been there for a year, and the number of operations I was doing unassisted was increasing, as was my salary. At home I knew I needed some help with Iris's problems, especially with getting her a driver's license. I was able to enlist Libby, from the office, to help teach her. Iris didn't feel that she needed anyone to push her to learn. However, I didn't want to start an argument by pointing out she hadn't opened the driver's manual.

Arriving home from work one evening, I was greeted by some good news.

"I got job and start tomorrow. I go into store and manager like me very much and he say he start me out and teach me what I have to know. It going to be hard for me. It every night from six to ten. I hope I able to do it till I go to school."

"Those are terrible hours. Just when I arrive, you'll be leaving. Didn't they have anything else?" I said.

Iris raised her voice. "You want me to get a job. This is what they give me. Now you no like it. What with you?"

She is right. I am being difficult.

"Okay, okay, try it. Maybe they'll switch you to different hours if they like you."

The next evening I drove her to work, which was only across the street from our apartment. I kissed her goodbye. "Don't be nervous, you'll be fine. You're a very smart girl. The learning of American money will come."

I watched as she left the car and walked into the mall, my eyes following my tall, attractive wife. With a strong step and long blond hair swaying side to side, she slowly disappeared into the shopping center. I hoped she would find some success in this small achievement.

At 10:00 p.m. I picked Iris up and couldn't wait to hear her assessment of the new job. I didn't have to wait long.

"Bob, this job for idiots," she said, climbing into the car with a huff.

I was dumbfounded. "What do you mean for idiots? You've only been there one night. How do you know it's a job for idiots?"

Iris slapped her hands on her lap as she turned toward me and yelled in my ear. "All I do is fold clothes all day, it stupid job. It not job for me. People there stupid. Girl that there give me orders, and she dope. I not listen to her. She stupid!"

"Why is she stupid? Because she tells you what to do? One day and you think you are the manager?" I said angrily.

"No, because she not know what she doing herself. Only a fool work there all day, folding, then unfolding clothes. First, she tell me put something here, then she tell me put it there. I think I going to quit."

"Like hell you're going to quit. You want to call your parents. You want new clothes. You want to run up bills, but you don't want to work," I said raising my voice.

"I not care, money not everything to me. I not be fool in this job, and I not going to stay if I feel like one."

"Now listen, lady, you quit this job and you're in big trouble."

"What are you going to do? You no make me go to job I no want."

"Damn it!" I said, realizing there was little I could do to make her stay. "Okay, at least give it two weeks, maybe it will get better. I don't want you sitting home every day."

Iris waited a second and then in a low tone, as if she was sacrificing herself, answered: "Two weeks, that all I work, no more."

We went to bed that night, but not before I had fulfilled Iris's request to kiss and hold her until she fell asleep. I listened to the muffled sounds of her crying.

Maybe I am expecting too much. She's just nineteen. Be patient. Think about what she gave up for you.

I had promised Iris we would go to Avi and Carmella's place the next day. We drove out to the west side of town, where they lived in a mobile home. It looked like a frontier home, isolated on the barren terrain, engulfed in a temporary sandstorm. I had briefly met Carmella before, when she had come to take Iris out. She was an attractive, soft-spoken woman with a good sense of humor.

She introduced me to her husband, Avi.

"How are you, Bob? It's good to meet you." Avi said, grabbing my hand and pumping it. He was a tall, muscular person who choked my fingers in a tight handshake. His accented voice was so loud that I thought someone may have mistakenly told him I was deaf. However, it became clear this was the way he talked to everyone.

"Here, I show you the place. There not much to see," Avi said as he took me on a tour of the trailer home. It was their son's fourth birthday. The trailer was filled with people who crowded into any available space. Avi led me along as I stepped over and on some of the people. He was an excellent host, seeming to talk with all the people present at the same time.

After the fifteen-second tour I found a small space on the floor and nestled in. Avi commanded the afternoon's conversation.

"Yes, me and Carmella left Israel for Colombia and become

fishermen. It not easy 'cause I know nothing about fishing. But I learn quickly, and soon we doing very well," he explained.

I was in disbelief. "You mean you went to South America without any idea how you were to earn money? Weren't you a bit frightened?"

Avi waved his hand at me. "No, no, not at all. I knew I could do something. It was just a matter of time. No, no, I was not scared. Carmella was a little bit frightened, but it not take long before we settled down. I do very well in short time. I have shrimp boat and people working for me. There very little to it, really."

"How the hell did you end up in Texas? Unless I missed something. The sea and the shrimp have been gone from the Permian Basin for a few thousand years."

"Oh, I meet person in Colombia from Odessa, and he invite me here and tell me he give me job, so I come here to work. So far, things been very good. I think we spend year or two, but we plan to go back to Israel," Avi thundered.

Carmella and Iris were preparing falafel for the guests. I felt like an underachiever as I listened to Avi tell his stories about the various wars he had taken part in back in Israel. He had fought and killed to protect his family on the kibbutz. Here was a man who had not only fought for his life but also challenged insecurity and the unknown in his adventures around the world.

On the drive home Iris asked me what I thought of Avi and Carmella. "Oh, I think they're very nice people. Avi seems a little pushy, as if there is nothing that can get in his way or bring him down. It frightens me when people are unafraid of anything although I must admit he has accomplished a lot."

If I was in awe, Iris was not. "Oh, he typical of all Israelis. They seem to feel they able to do anything. They all like little gods. It make me sick."

It was a surprise to me that the qualities I admired Iris thought so little of.

"I tired of people like that. They feel they know everything but they don't. But still, they very nice people and I like them a lot. Carmella very good friend and I feel happy when I talk to her. I hope we can come again," Iris said.

I kept my eyes on the road and adjusted the air conditioner to full blast in the Texas June heat. "Yes, certainly, if they're your friends, we will come again. I don't know that Avi and I have much in common, but perhaps we can find something to do together. You wanted to go to temple with them, so let's do that next week."

"Yes, I want to see if it as funny as Carmella say."

"That's not nice, you want to go just to laugh. Don't you want to meet other Jewish people?" I said.

"No, I not believe it necessary to pray. I no need to go to temple to meet people. I feel people not need religion all the time, that it not good for them. It no matter where I make friends. People not need religion, they all the same. Religion make people stand out differently. I want friends who think same as me not because they same religion."

"I think you're in for a big surprise here. You're in an area where very few people are Jewish, you're gonna stick out. People here have never seen a Jew. They certainly know nothing about Jewish heritage, and I think many believe Israel is somewhere close to New Jersey. You're going to want to meet Jewish people, even if you don't think so," I said.

Iris shrugged. "We'll see, we'll see," she muttered.

* * *

It was unrealistic to expect Iris to compete in college without the necessary fundamental skills. We went down to the local college, The University of Texas of the Permian Basin, to enroll her in some preparatory courses for the summer as a non-matriculated student. She was ecstatic about attending. However, the first hurdle to cross was getting her driver's license so she could get to class. Libby had done an excellent job teaching her to drive, and I hardly had one complaint when Iris drove us to the motor vehicle department so she could take her road test.

I waited as she went with the examiner. When she was done, she got out of the car and threw her arms around me.

"I pass, I pass. I make some mistakes, but he say I do enough right to pass. I go in now and get picture taken. You wait," she said as she turned and ran back to the office.

There was such a look of accomplishment on her face that it struck me as ironic that what I took for granted she considered a great prize. In Israel, obtaining a driver's license was something of a small miracle. It required teaching from a government-certified instructor, which was quite an expense. In Iris's mind, getting this license was a real feat. I was relieved to know she could now leave the apartment without me. This would open the way to new friendships and diversions from her present confinement.

That Friday we went with Avi and Carmella to the temple for services. Avi, in a brief time, had already met most of the Jewish people in the area. Because of his good humor and friendliness, he was on a first-name basis with everyone.

Iris turned to me. "Bob, don't you know these people?" she said as she held my hand.

I looked around the room. "I recognize most of them, but I don't know any of them very well. I'd like to introduce you to them, but unfortunately, I don't know their names," I said sheepishly.

We walked up to some people whose faces I recognized. Because I didn't know their names, all I could do was shove Iris in front of me and introduce her as my wife. I then stepped back and let Iris fend for herself. Iris, like a seasoned politician, would step forward and extend her hand; her brilliant smile could eclipse the sun.

"I very happy to meet you," she would say as I hid in the background. Whoever she was talking to would introduce themselves, and I could then reenter the conversation.

"How come you not know people here when you here one year and Avi know everybody and he here two months?" Iris asked.

"That's a good question, to which I have a lousy answer, so I'll just keep it to myself. Let's go pray," I said, leading her to our seats.

The services started, alternating between English and Hebrew. Iris and Carmella competed with the service as they sat laughing and giggling. Finally, when I had had enough of the interruptions, I took Iris's arm firmly and spoke into her ear.

"Iris, stop this laughing, it's embarrassing. If you're not interested, shut up and let other people listen."

"I no help it, it very funny to me," she said.

"Well, it's not funny to me. Go out if you want to laugh," I said, turning back to my prayer book.

When the services ended, we stayed to mingle with the crowd. Avi and Carmella did most of introducing Iris to the people. She fluttered from one to the other with a smile and handshake. Most people asked where she was from and how long she had been here. When she told them she had come as the wife of Dr. Jaffee, they looked perplexed. I suppose I was still a hidden commodity in the community.

We said goodbye to Avi and Carmella and returned home.

I was still angry at Iris for laughing during the services and asked her what was so funny.

"I no help it. Carmella right, this not religious. It all English of no meaning," she said as we entered our apartment

I stopped to look at her. "How would you know? You never went to temple in Israel."

Iris slapped her hands against her thighs. "Don't be stupid. I not go to temple often, but I go enough to know that *this* not temple. It stupid to have temple like this. It better they have nothing."

"That's ridiculous. It doesn't make any difference how people pray if they feel comfortable doing it. Just because they don't know Hebrew and pray in English doesn't mean they should not pray," I said.

Iris sighed. "I not know. I just know this not temple. It just place where people act like fools."

It was obvious the temple was not going to be an important part of her life. I felt she would come to regret her inability to see that being Jewish was more than just being born Jewish.

She didn't know how many people harbored feelings of anti-Semitism. It could be subtle, like, "I'll Jew the price down," or overt, like "You're a Jew bastard." She had never experienced this in Israel, but I had here in the States. I felt it was only a matter of time before she did as well.

CHAPTER THIRTY-TWO
School Begins

*I*t was eight days later and a Saturday. As on most Saturdays Iris was calling Israel. I was finally learning to be more understanding by not saying a word while she was on the phone. Iris was also learning, cutting her conversations in half. As she always spoke in Hebrew, I could not understand the conversation. When I asked her what she had talked about, she would decline to answer, saying, "It was nothing much," adding that if I really wanted to know, I should learn Hebrew.

"Now Iris, what am I going to do with Hebrew?"

"It something you should learn so you able to talk to me," she said calmly.

I just could see no logic in that. "I realize trying to get through to you in English is difficult, but I think if I try to make conversation in

Hebrew it will be impossible. Besides, it would take me years to learn Hebrew, and who would I use it with except you?"

"It something you have to know for our children. I going to teach our children Hebrew and send them to Israel. So, if you want to talk to children too, you learn Hebrew." She began to make dinner.

I felt our children would certainly learn English before Hebrew, but it was premature to argue. "Well, right now, we don't have a kid, so I don't have to worry."

"This something we should settle right now. When we have children, there no doubt that they go to Israel to live for several years. They going to know Hebrew too. Now if you want to learn Hebrew, I think it good but it make no difference to me 'cause I going to treat children the same," Iris said firmly.

"When you live here for a while and become more American, you will change your mind. I think you will think less strongly about sending our children to Israel and teaching them Hebrew," I said.

Iris threw up her hands, shook her head and raised her voice. "No, no, this I never change. They will understand. This no discussion. I no think I ever become American."

It was obvious she wanted to hang onto her old identity as long as possible. It was security for her, but I thought this just a passing desire on her part, fading as she became more acclimated to American society. "Well, we'll see. Perhaps you can start teaching me a little Hebrew and see what progress I make. And maybe we will retire to Israel to live, but right now, eat, or you will be late for work."

I had not made any progress in finding Iris a new job, and she had not changed her mind about quitting her present one. She arrived home that evening and again launched into a tirade about the mental abuse she was taking at work.

"Bob, you have no idea how stupid people are there. Sixteen-year-old girl ask what to do with boyfriend. She say she getting raped in backseat of car and want to know if she should go out with boyfriend this week. How people so stupid? If she not have sense to say no, what she want advice from me for? How I able to work with people like this?" she complained. Iris extended her arms to their full width. "And you no believe boss either. They change boss there every day because each one too stupid to last more than two days. New one today spend all time putting on makeup so she look good when she go out. She not care about store at all. Only when she think she get yelled at because store a mess does she give me lots of orders and then go back to makeup again. And she ugly! I be glad when I leave."

It all sounded amusing to me. "I don't know, it sounds kind of interesting, being the psychiatrist to a sixteen-year-old."

"Oh, Bob, it silly and you know it. Not only that, but man follow me around store and ask me out. He not buy anything, just bother me the whole day. So, you see I have to quit right away."

I was still not serious. "I don't know, Iris, I think I would only quit if he was not good-looking or rich. But if he's six feet tall and owns a lot of oil wells, I would stay on the job."

I looked up in time to see a pillow flying in my direction. Iris rose from the sofa and walked off. Halfway across the living room, she turned and smiled.

"He was very handsome. I don't know if he rich, but he very good-looking, and he not have big nose like you." She then continued to the bedroom.

Two days later she quit her job.

* * *

A few weeks later Iris started school. It was July 1980; Iris had been in Odessa for four months and had turned twenty. She dressed for class and stood in front of the mirror as I looked on. She was trying on a multitude of outfits, which all landed on the floor. I could hardly find the rug in the mess. She was oblivious to it, claiming she had nothing to wear and needed new clothes.

"Pick up your clothes. We're not pigs here," I said, looking at all the garments scattered around the room.

"Now, Bob, this is the way I get dressed. If you want to know I such a mess you should have asked me before we marry, and I would have told you. Since you not ask me, you have nothing to be upset about."

She has a point.

I smiled to myself as I gingerly picked my way to the bathroom.

"Bob, come out of there. I be late for school, and I want to kiss you goodbye."

I stepped out of the bathroom, gave her a kiss and some reassurance. "I'm sure you'll do fine at school. You can't be as dumb as me, and I got through. I'll see you later. Be good."

* * *

When I came home that evening, she was asleep on the sofa. Beside her was a pile of unopened books, most still in their plastic wrappers. I bent down and kissed Iris on the cheek, awakening her.

"Well, how is the student doing?" I said, looking at all the books on the floor. "By the looks of all these books, you should be on your way to being Shakespeare in no time."

Iris buried her chin in my chest. "It hopeless. I not able to do this," she muttered.

"You've only been to school one day and you're giving up? What's the matter with you? Of course you can't expect everything to go right the first day. If you knew everything, then you wouldn't need to go to school."

She sat up. "It too difficult. I sit down with teacher, but I no see how I ever learn English well enough to go to school. I not even able to write a sentence. How I able to write papers?"

I raised my voice. "Stop this! I'm tired of hearing you give up. You give up your job, you give up school, you give up everything and go back to Israel. Now listen, you're not going to give up. You may eventually fail, but you're at least going to put some effort into trying." I reached down to pick up one of her books. "Now what do you have to do for tomorrow? Show me, and I'll help you do it."

Iris took the book out of my hand. "No, no you not able to do homework for me, and I not able to do it myself," she yelled.

I calmed down, seeing how desperate she had become. "I didn't say I was going to do the homework for you, I said I would help you do it. Now show me what you have to do," I said in a softer tone.

Iris took the English textbook from the floor and showed me the assigned lessons.

I looked at the lessons. "Now this doesn't look that hard, finding the subject and predicate, the components of a sentence. You read this now, and I'll help you later."

Grammar was one of my worst subjects. However, it didn't make much sense to try to cheer her up by telling her, after spending my entire life speaking English, I couldn't do her homework either. But she felt better just knowing there was someone who would try to help her.

While Iris was attempting to read her homework in the living room, I went to the bedroom and called Steven.

"It's tough being married," I said.

I could hear Steven laughing. "Yeah, I know how you feel. With all that young pussy going around and you have to go home to the same woman every night. Not like the old days, when you just screwed anything you saw. Although in your case, it was probably more wishful thinking."

I wasn't laughing. "Well, it's not that. I don't know if Iris is going to be happy here, and if she ain't happy, I'm not happy."

"Are you still having to do the laundry and cook the dinners?" Steven asked.

I let it all out. "Yes, and not only that. She cries herself to sleep every night. I don't know what to do with her. I try to find her friends, but she doesn't like most people here."

Steven's tone softened. "Look, Bob, just take it easy. Give it some time and she'll adjust. Remember the sacrifice she made. This woman gave up her country, her family, her friends to be with you. But when you reach a point that you and Iris feel that it's not going to work out, then you may have to make some other plans. But for the present I would not get excited."

"But I have my work that demands so much of my time. Now I have to do her homework."

"Give the girl a break. You are her husband. You're not supposed to spend all your time studying. Do the best you can and talk it over with her. If after several months it doesn't work out, then you will have to make some new decisions, but for now, don't be angry. Be more considerate."

After we concluded the call, I went back to the living room to find Iris closing her books after only fifteen minutes. She said she was tired and was going to bed.

I held her in bed, in the dark silence interrupted by her soft crying.

"Iris, what's wrong? Tell me what's wrong." I asked.

Iris just shook her head and continued to cry.

"How can I help you if you don't tell me anything?"

Again, no answer.

"If you're not going to tell me what's wrong. I'm not going to listen to you cry."

Frustrated, I turned my back on her and went to sleep.

It will only be a matter of time before the end of our marriage. I am sure Iris will be returning to Israel.

I wanted her to be happy, to stop crying, to have the inner strength to conquer her problems. I did not feel I could solve her loneliness, especially when she would not verbalize her feelings to me. My responses were inadequate, my beliefs stubborn.

Why am I failing her?

CHAPTER THIRTY-THREE
Surprise

The weather became extremely hot as August approached. Iris was continuing with her basic English course at school. Coming home for lunch one day, I found Iris sunbathing by the pool.

"Bob, it ten minutes after twelve. How come you late for lunch?" Iris said, sitting up and placing her hands on her hips.

I came forward to kiss her. "Believe me, it was very difficult visiting my mistress for only ten minutes."

Iris rose from her chair and reached for my hand. "You laugh, but I worry if you not come on time. I think maybe something bad happen to you."

I held Iris and kissed her again as we entered the apartment. Spread over the sofa were her books. I looked at the notebooks in her handwriting. Mostly in Hebrew with an occasional word of English repeated numerous times. I asked her what it said.

She peeked out from the kitchen. "Oh, that my homework."

I looked at the paper front and back, right side up and upside down, or what I thought was up and down.

"Iris is that what you hand in?" I said, holding the paper by its edge outstretched in front of me.

"No, it just for me to practice on and this the way I do it."

I put the paper back on the sofa. "That's very good, but I think you should do more in English. I don't think your teachers are fluent in Hebrew."

Iris banged a plate hard onto the table. "You stop it. I just practice. I still think in Hebrew first, then English."

I sat down at the table as Iris brought out sandwiches for lunch.

"I try and then I see. I not know how I do, but I start. It very difficult," she said hopefully.

As I got up, I noticed she had done all the laundry and cleaned the house. I complimented her.

"Yes, I do it all. It not take long."

"That's great. It would take me the whole day to clean the apartment. Maybe you're getting the hang of being a housewife."

Iris shook her head. "No, no, I never like doing it, that why I so quick in getting it done. Also, I need something to clean floor with. Floor dirty and you not have anything."

"Oh, you mean a vacuum cleaner." I said as I put my arm around her. "There is so much wind in west Texas I thought it would just blow the dirt away if I opened the door. But I'll get one."

I headed out the door toward my car to go back to work.

Iris stood at the door and called, "When you be home?"

Getting into my car, I called back: "About five or six."

In a distant, fading voice I heard, "Now don't you be late. I be waiting."

As I drove back to the office, I was happy that Iris was at least trying to do the schoolwork. She was even cleaning the house.

Maybe there is hope this will work out. There's a long way to go, but progress is being made. Will it continue? Will it be enough?

* * *

Lillie called on the following Saturday. Although Lillie was Iris's only blood relative in the country, Iris did not talk to her often. She thought Lillie was too dictatorial and pushy.

Lillie and Iris spoke in Hebrew, which left me out of the conversation. I had not heard from Lillie in some time and was not eager to talk to her, feeling that Iris must have told her that life was not going smoothly.

But eventually Iris handed me the phone.

"How is everything in Odessa? How is your surgery coming?" Lillie asked.

"It's coming very well. I get to do a lot of cases, and I'm doing all right financially. Iris just bought some new clothes, so you can feel assured that I'm making enough that she doesn't have to dress in rags." I could understand that Lillie was concerned about Iris. I wanted Lillie to know I was trying to take care of her niece. Lillie's next statement came as a bombshell to me.

"I've just spoken to Sarah and Ziggy. They say they will be coming to the US next month to visit."

Oh, God! They too want to see that I'm not beating their daughter.

I didn't know what to say. My immediate response was that Iris and I needed more time to work out our problems before we had the additional burden of her parents' visit. Naturally, they would take Iris's side in any dispute. I still felt Iris needed to take on more responsibilities for the house. She needed more time to adapt to the US, to me, to school. Her parents would only influence her to take the easy way out and return to Israel. I was afraid that maybe that would be the best course for her.

Regaining my composure, I said to Lillie, "Well, that's very nice. I'm sure Iris will be delighted."

After we hung up, I sat by the phone for a minute. How could I tell Lillie or anybody how unhappy Iris was? How can you adjust a culture to fit the expectations of a twenty-year-old girl? How could

I tell anyone how, after only five months of marriage, Iris wanted to throw in the towel and go back to Israel? I knew there would be troubles and times of despair in a marriage, but how could I correct the inherent aloofness Iris had for an entire society? I thought marital fights were supposed to be about buying furniture or about what clothes to wear when going out. Our problems were a low fog of constant despair and discouragement.

My thoughts were interrupted as Iris entered the room.

"Bob, Bob, you hear my parents come to see me in a month? I so happy."

I wanted to say that this would not change anything, that our problems of yesterday and today would be problems she had when they were here and when they left. But maybe the parents could talk to Iris about the difficulties of marriage. Maybe they could make her try a little harder to adjust.

Maybe they would end up taking her back with them.

Seeing Iris so happy, I could not discourage her.

I lied. "Yes, I think it's great. Fantastic. I don't know what we will do with your parents here, but I'll look for a few places for them to go so they don't die of boredom."

"Oh, it not necessary. They come to see me. I sure they just be happy to see me and I to see them. I so happy I not know what to do." She put her arms around me and started hugging and kissing me, pushing me onto the bed with her.

She is so happy to be with her parents, so miserable in the US. How could she resist not returning to Israel? Maybe that would be the best for both of us. But no, I can't give up this early. I remember how she consoled me, how we talked, laughed, how much she loves and cares for me. These are such good things. I cannot throw them away without trying harder to make her stay.

CHAPTER THIRTY-FOUR
It Won't Work

O n Monday at work I asked Dr. Sheets if he was interested in hiring another ophthalmologist at the clinic. Steven hated Monticello and thought his potential wasn't realized in that small town. He asked if there was an opportunity in Odessa for him. The clinic had four ophthalmologists and two optometrists, but we were still busy. It was possible there was room for another ophthalmologist.

Dr. Sheets stroked his chin as he said, "Well, I can't promise anything, but it is not out of the question that we hire another person. If your brother wants to come down here and take another look, I certainly wouldn't have any objections. We can talk to him and sort of get the lay of the land and take it from there. What do you think about working with your brother?"

Now it was time for me to rub my chin. "I know my brother is an excellent ophthalmologist. I've worked with him, and I can say without hesitation that he is an excellent doctor. The only thing we had serious difficulty with was business. However, since we won't be in direct competition as far as salary is concerned, I don't see that as a problem."

Dr. Sheets was a man who thought a lot but let little out through his lips. "Well, let me know when your brother comes down, and we can get together and talk." He rose from his chair like some huge, dominant beast of the water hole, left his office, and went to see his next patient.

I went home that evening knowing that Iris would not take this news very well. I didn't know what would happen if Steven and I worked together under Sheets. I felt we could get along socially, but also thought Steven would never be happy working for someone. Being in this clinic, he would never be the boss. Would he still have the need to dominate me even if we were both salaried employees? Would he always have to feel that he was the better ophthalmologist? Would I be willing to work for less than him if he claimed he had more experience? I was unsure, but I still loved my brother and had an affinity for working with him.

That evening I told Iris about Steven coming to Odessa. Her reaction did not surprise me, although I felt with time it would change.

"It not good. It not good," Iris said, shaking her head. She got up from her chair and went into the kitchen. "Bob, it not work. You told me about you and brother not get along in past, and you will not get along in future. He come here and he take you over. I not going to be second to your brother. I wish you understand I say this because I love you so much that I not want to see you hurt. You better than brother, you not need him. You able to do it on your own. I tell you this before and I tell you again."

Iris stood in the kitchen, aimlessly doing nothing. I got up and joined her. I thought she was exaggerating the hold Steven had over me. He was no Svengali, no magic sorcerer.

"Iris, don't get so upset about this. First, I don't know if Steven will want to come here or whether he could reach an agreement with Sheets. Two, even if he does come here, he and I will not be business partners. We will both be working for the big boss, Dr. Sheets. Also, I was the first down here, and I don't see him pushing me out of the way. A lot has changed since we worked together. I am a much better ophthalmologist than I was when I was with him. I just don't see him dominating—"

Iris again shook her head. "You no understand. It not make difference whether he own practice or not own practice. You no see that he always tell you what to do, that he always be big brother over you. It not make difference where you are or what type of relation you have with him, he always want to be boss and you will always follow him. This not for me. If you and him want to be in business together then you make decision, but I make my decision. I no stay here if he come." She brushed past me and went into the bedroom.

I followed her, feeling that I could still convince her. "Iris, just give me a second."

"*Sheket, sheket, dai, dai*" ("quiet, quiet, enough, enough"), she said.

When Iris spoke to me in Hebrew, I knew the conversation was over. She looked down, folded some clothes, and placed them in the dresser. As Iris rarely folded anything, I could tell she was upset. I went over and kissed her on the neck. She turned toward me for a second, then shook herself loose.

After dinner in silence, she abruptly got up, went to the bedroom, and fell asleep.

She certainly is looking out for me. Maybe she is right, I should give up working with Steven and concentrate on my own career. Maybe she sees something I don't see. It would always be impossible to be in business with Steven.

CHAPTER THIRTY-FIVE
Ups and Downs

*T*he next morning being my surgical day, I awakened early for the hospital.

After surgery I went home. I didn't want to eat lunch. All I wanted to do was forget the morning. I climbed into bed and went to sleep. Iris, upon returning from school for lunch, came into the bedroom.

"Bob, wake up. What the matter with you?" Iris demanded as she tried to pull the covers away from me.

"You're married to a klutz, a real klutz," I replied.

Iris of course had no idea what had occurred that morning. She again asked what was wrong.

I rolled over like some dying whale to present my soliloquy. "Your husband is a dope. I went in this morning to do a case using that new technique and made a mess of everything; now the guy probably will not see anything, in what should have been an easy case. I'm an idiot!" I yelled the last few words as I pulled the covers over my head. "There is only one thing for me to do and that is to bury myself here until I die. I think I'll just wait until I die of starvation."

Through the covers I could hear Iris laughing.

"Bob, I no want you to lie there and die, 'cause then you start to smell and I not able to sleep next to you."

My tone changed as I came back to reality. "Now, don't laugh. I screwed up somebody's eye, hardly something to laugh about."

Iris put her arms around me and kissed me on the cheek. "I sorry to see you so sad. You know you do the best you can. If you operate, every time not going to be perfect, sometimes things go wrong. This not mean you bad."

I was still feeling remorse for the patient and self-pity. "But, Iris, the people that come to me are paying me for my service. They have a right to expect that I'm not going to screw it all up. I really screwed this one up good." I said, beating my head against the pillow.

"You do what you thought was right. You didn't try to do bad job on his eye. Now you can't sit here and blame yourself."

"Tell that to the patient when he loses his vision. Tell him I did the best I could," I shouted.

Iris didn't respond further. She just climbed into bed and put her arms around me while we both fell asleep bathed in the afternoon sun.

* * *

The next day the patient did not look as bad as I feared nor as good as I hoped. My guilt made it difficult to keep up the appearance of an optimistic attitude while examining him. I wanted to just confess my mistakes to him and ask for his forgiveness. Whatever was churning inside of me, I tried to keep my words as calm and upbeat as possible. There was nothing to be done now except wait and see how the eye healed. I wished I could go to sleep for three months and wake up knowing the result. Just the thought of looking each day at this eye I had damaged made me sick, and I'm sure the patient felt the same, although he did not express it.

When I arrived home that day, Iris was quick to ask how the patient was doing. I suppose the look on my face expressed my feelings.

"Now Bob, maybe he do better than you think. I know you try to do everything you can. It no do you good to just worry all the time, it not make him better. It no do you good even if you kill yourself—it done now," Iris said, like an old sage.

I held my head in my hands and slumped into a chair, still feeling shame for the harm done to my patient. I couldn't get over the fact that it was my hands that caused the complication. But Iris was right, there was no use dwelling on it.

Iris might have a twenty-year-old body, but she has a fifty-year-old mind. How'd she get so smart?

Changing the subject, she declared, "I not able to make anything for dinner 'cause there nothing in house to eat."

Already upset at myself over my surgical complication, it didn't take much to add more fuel to my anger. "What do you mean there is nothing in the house? You have a car and a license. Why didn't you go out and get something?"

Iris put her hands on her hips in a combative stance. "Now you know I don't want to go alone. If you want to eat you go with me. This something we share. Now you make up your mind." Iris threw herself down on the sofa and began to read one of her schoolbooks.

"Oh, screw it, let's go," I said angrily as I grabbed the car keys and walked outside.

We drove to the grocery store in silence. In the store, I took a shopping cart and headed down the aisles. There was no use asking Iris what we needed since I felt she didn't know. Iris just shuffled along behind me, picking up a can here and a vegetable there, placing it in the cart. We went separate ways in the store, grabbing produce. Meeting at the shopping cart, we looked at each other, noticing that we were both carrying the same items, a bag of tomatoes and a can of soup. Again, viewing the cart, we saw there were duplicates of almost all the items. We burst into laughter.

Like one mind with four feet.

"Now, Iris, who's going to eat all these tomatoes?" I asked gesticulating with my head. Iris continued to laugh. Her smile was so wide and warm, it could have stewed the tomatoes in their bags. She composed herself and told me to just push the cart and she would fill it. As I stood thinking of a reply, Iris moved closer and kissed me on the cheek.

"Bob, I love you—now kiss me."

"Here in the store, with all these people around?"

"Oh, who care?" She put one arm around me and squeezed me between herself and the tomatoes. Now with mushy tomatoes, we walked down the aisle, Iris picking up groceries while I brought up the rear with the cart.

"Bob, today they call me from the temple and ask me if I could teach Hebrew to the children," Iris said, reaching for a chicken.

"I think that will be great. It will get you out of the house, and besides, you enjoy children, so I think it will be good for you to do."

"I don't know. I so busy with school I don't know if I will have time. It would be one hour on Sunday morning."

This didn't sound like it would be much of a sacrifice, so I encouraged Iris to at least try it as she could always quit.

Arriving back at the apartment, we unpacked the groceries, and I then went back to studying. After a few minutes Iris came to me.

"Why you no talk to me? You not help me and you not even say anything to me," she said.

I looked up from my book. "I have work to do. I just can't go with you all day shopping and then spend the evening goofing off. I must do this work."

Iris stood over me, hands on her hips. "Every night you come home, you do work. When you going to have time to be married?"

I forcibly closed my book. "This is the work I must do for my patients. Try to understand. This is what it is like to be married to a doctor. Would you rather I be a second-rate doctor?"

Iris took a seat on the sofa. "I rather you be a first-rate husband."

She opened her books to do her assignment. I went back to my reading. Finishing an hour later, I noticed that Iris was still working on her homework. There were papers scattered all over the floor. I walked over and picked one up. It was filled with repetitions of a single word in English. I bent down to kiss her on the cheek.

She pulled away. "No, you too busy to have wife. You go back to work."

"Now, be fair. I have to do this reading . I get seven medical magazines a month to read. Now, understand."

Iris, as if she didn't hear a word, just continued writing. "I not like anything. I come here to be wife, not to sit in corner and be quiet. You make up mind if you want wife or not."

I reassured Iris that of course I wanted her as my wife. I turned her head toward me and tried to kiss her. But she was stubborn and pulled away. I wanted to get her attention and felt making her laugh would help.

"Well, if you're not going to talk to me, there is only one thing left for me to do and that is lay down here and die," I said, placing myself on the rug. I covered myself with the scattered papers that were on the floor. My hands and feet were in the air, and to be sure she noticed, I started to groan. Finally, Iris closed her book and stood above me.

"Bob, you crazy! Look at mess you make. What the matter with you? You nut!"

I pulled the papers off my face. "No, I just want to get the attention of the one I love."

"If you want to get attention of one you love, then it better that you give her time and talk to her than act like some nut," she said as she turned and headed to the bathroom.

It was going to take more time for me to get adjusted to being married. I made no headway that evening, as she again cried herself to sleep.

I have a lot to learn about being a husband.

CHAPTER THIRTY-SIX
A New Interest

The summer was ending. It was September 1980, and Iris had been in the United States for six months. She had taken a basic English course over the summer and now re-enrolled at the college for a full semester. She decided to try photography and journalism. Her courses also included continuation of basic English.

With the fall came the hunting season for quail in Odessa. Coming from New York City, I was not an experienced hunter but wanted the opportunity to try. Besides, I enjoyed eating quail.

I had an invitation from Charles to go hunting and gladly accepted. Although I initially wanted to go alone, Iris would hear none of it. She demanded to go.

Back at work I told Charles that Iris was going hunting with us.

"Now, Bob, you have to tell your wife that she can't go. You must be firm. If you let her get away with this at the beginning of the marriage, she will just keep taking. Now, show her who's boss," Charles said, placing his hand on my back for added emphasis.

"Look, it's not so terrible that she comes along. She wouldn't let me go by myself because she doesn't want to be home alone, so I'm going to have to take her with us. I tried to explain to her that she might not like going, but she said if she doesn't go, I don't go, so I guess I had better like her going."

Charles was adamant. "Now that's what I mean, you have got to show her who runs the house. The bible says that the man is owner of his abode. If you don't assert yourself, you're going to be like some old doormat that is walked on constantly. Now, I want you to go back and tell her she can't go. Why, if this came up in my marriage, I would just tell Mary she couldn't go and that would be that, not all this discussion."

I was resigned to my fate. "Charles, I don't think anything will happen with her coming. She probably knows more about guns then I do, having been in the Israeli army. So, I'm not going to start a fight over it. I'm just going to have her come."

Charles just shook his head. I guess he was unable to understand this betrayal of manhood and religion. "Okay, just don't say I didn't warn you. She's telling you what to do and you're letting her get away with it. When she has you doing the housework and begging for a day off, don't say I didn't tell you," Charles said, leaving the room as his words hit the floor behind him.

* * *

Iris was wrestling with her schoolwork. She would complain that she was unable to do the assignments and then go back and try again. I was falling further behind in my work. It was difficult to keep up with all the journals while trying to break Iris in. After seven months in the States, she still had few friends.

A few days after my discussion with Charles, I came back to the apartment to find Iris asleep. I took the opportunity to start reading the stack of medical magazines accumulating. Iris awoke and called from the bedroom. "Bob, is that you?"

"Yes, I'm here. How was your day at school?" I answered, getting up and walking into the bedroom. I sat down next to her and she put her arms around me.

"Oh, Bob, I love photography. It wonderful. I think I like it very much. The teacher, he very nice to me, he ask each of us a little bit about ourselves. I tell him I from Israel, he seem very interested. I think this going to be what I like," Iris said, beaming with enthusiasm.

She was not happy with her other courses. She felt English and journalism were too difficult, but she would try it. I was glad she found something that she could enjoy. I kissed her and went back to the living room and my journals. A few minutes later Iris approached with the camera I had given her.

"Bob, show me how camera works," she said, pulling the various knobs on it.

I tried to explain that I was busy presently and asked her to read the instruction manual. If she had questions, I would help her later.

"When you have time for me? Don't help me, it okay, just forget it." Iris dropped the camera on the sofa and went to the dining-room table to sit.

I put my journal down and turned to speak to her. "Now, I've got this work to do. I didn't say I wouldn't help you. "Don't get so upset," I said half apologetically, half angrily. "I just don't have time right now. Give me a chance to do some of my own work."

"*Dai, dai*, Bob," Iris said keeping her head in her books and giving me the palm of her hand as a reply.

"Now Iris, don't be like that. Come here," I commanded. "Come here, I'll show you how this goddamn camera works."

"No, leave me alone," she said.

I had not calmed down. "As long as you've already bothered me, I might as well show you how this thing works."

"Bob, *dai, dai*."

I walked over to her and looked down over her shoulder. There were tears coming down her cheeks. I put my arms around her shoulders and rubbed her neck slightly as I looked up to gather my own feelings—as if I wanted to forge a path through the forest, I now found all the trees burnt down. I took her support and sympathy but was not willing to give her equal consideration. I knew Iris well enough to know that being so hurt, she would withdraw into herself.

She dried her eyes, got up, and went to the bedroom to lie down in bed. When I went to her, she just buried her head deeper into the pillow. I tried to explain that I was sorry, I just wanted to catch up with my own work and not hurt her. I don't know what she understood, as in silence the tears continued down her face. I couldn't accomplish much reading that evening.

Another day in a failing marriage.

CHAPTER THIRTY-SEVEN
The Medical Party

*I*t was October 1980. Dr. Sheets had decided another ophthalmologist was not needed. Steven would have to remain in Monticello for the present. Naturally, Iris was not disappointed.

We had also in October received an invitation to a party at the hospital. When the night of the party arrived, Iris carefully dressed.

"Bob, I not know what to wear. Do I dress fancy?"

"You will look good in anything. Don't worry about it," I said grabbing her waist and slapping her on her butt.

I looked at the floor, which she had redecorated with assorted colors of blouses, dresses, and pants. I also gazed at her legs. She was such a beautiful woman, it did not seem possible these vein-scarred legs were part of her. You could trace the veins like so many railroad tracks in a busy freight yard, crossing and crisscrossing.

"I can't wear dress 'cause my legs show and they not pretty, so I wear pants. That be okay?" she said while staring at the mirror, changing and re-changing. She flung her blond hair back behind her shoulders. "I not pretty, I ugly," she said, pulling at her blouse.

I could not believe that anyone who took such care in their dress would believe they weren't attractive. "You're very pretty: a beautiful face and a beautiful figure."

"But my legs terrible and my face have little bumps."

"Oh, stop it. You have only a few little, tiny spots on your face and your legs are fine, so forget about it. Let's go." I wrapped my hands around her waist, kissed her on the face and whispered in her ear: "I think you're the most beautiful woman in Odessa."

"Only in Odessa? Only Odessa?" Iris said, laughing.

We kissed and were off to the event.

It was a party for the medical department. I was not friendly with many of the doctors because they were older. If the people were older than me and I was twelve years older than Iris, she must really have felt out of place. I tried to introduce her to as many people as I could remember the names of, which were just a few. The rest I let come to us and introduce themselves. Iris stood with a glass of wine in her hand held high next to her face, arched her back and distributed her weight to her heels. The white wine was warm, so I put an ice cubes into the glass. When introduced to anyone, she would just move the glass away from the side of her mouth and light up a huge smile that blended into her blond hair.

Dr. John Smith came over and introduced himself. He was a fifty-five-year-old man with little hair and a lot of weight mounted on a short frame.

"Dr. and Mrs. Jaffee, my wife Nora," he said.

Nora interrupted. "Yes, I know Mrs. Jaffee. She and I are in the same photography class. I think we will have a very good time. You know, John, Mrs. Jaffee is from Israel."

"Oh, how nice," Dr. Smith said as he looked around the room for other acquaintances. "It must be quite a change, coming to this country."

Iris smiled again. "Yes." She then placed the glass back across her lips to cover her mouth.

Dr. Smith and his wife, realizing this conversation was going nowhere, nodded and passed on. Iris turned to me, moving the glass to the side.

"Bob, I not Mrs. I not wife. I Iris. Why not people call me Iris? That my name," she complained.

I just smiled and placed my hand on Iris's back to lead her along as I told her not to get excited about her name, which I pointed out no one even knew. She was still insistent.

"I not going to be called Mrs. for rest of my life."

We walked over to Dr. Gupta and his wife. I introduced Iris to her satisfaction.

Dr. Gupta looked Iris up and down. "Such a lovely wife. You are a fortunate man. This is my wife, Joan," he said.

Joan looked at Iris as if an alien had arrived. "How darling you are. You're just like one of my daughters, such a charming girl."

Iris moved the glass from her lips to give her usual smile. Simultaneously, I could hear the ice cubes in the glass rattle as Iris shook the glass. I knew it was time to leave.

"Bob, I have work to do. There is nothing here for me, they are too old for me. I have nothing to talk to them about. I waste time here."

It didn't seem I had much in common with the group either. Most of them had watches worth more than my entire assets. It was sort of funny to me as Iris did look young enough to be one of the doctors' daughters who had been allowed to stay up late. Iris was probably seething inside. She wasn't going to be a "Mrs." or a "doctor's wife," she was going to be something of her own making, an "Iris." She wasn't going to blend in with the crowd. If she didn't think she fit in, she was going to let me know. I admired that she was fighting so hard to prove her identity, whatever that was to be.

CHAPTER THIRTY-EIGHT
It's Impossible

*I*ris's initial enthusiasm for photography was waning, as the difficulty of reading the textbooks increased.

"Bob, what this word?" Iris said pointing to the word *daguerreotype*.

I explained that it was a process for making photographs in the 1840s and 1850s. Looking at her textbooks, I could see she had made notes in the margin, all in Hebrew. She was still most comfortable thinking in that language.

"I not think I do well in these tests. The teacher ask a lot from us and I not think I do well. Maybe if you explain a little I able to do it."

After watching her for a few minutes turning the pages back and forth at the speed of a hummingbird's wings, I sat beside her and started to read her book page by page to be able to regurgitate it back to her. I read about the daguerreotype, the ambrotype, and the tintype. I would explain each process to her after reading it in the book. She took notes, asking an occasional question.

"Oh, it make a little more sense to me now. I think I know what teacher trying to say," she said.

Iris moved closer to me and placed her hand on my lap. A smile came across her face; her skin was less taut, more relaxed.

It was already ten thirty by my watch. I went back to my reading, and Iris continued with her assignment. A few minutes later, she dropped her pen on the paper.

"I never able to do this right." She exhaled deeply.

I went over and noticed the word *daguerreotype* written over and over on a pad in English.

"Bob, look at this. I not able to write this word. How I able to pass if I not able to write one word? All these people in my class been here all their life. How I able to take test with them when I not understand and no write?"

It was easy for me to tell Iris to be confident when I knew under similar circumstances in Israel, I would be unable to compete. "Now, look, you may not get the best marks in the class, but you can do it. The next semester you'll do better and the term after that, better still. It's tough— sure, it's tough, but it's not impossible. I'll help, but you must have the will to keep going, to keep trying even if at times it seems impossible."

She looked up at me imploring, "I not even able to say this one word *da-guerr-eo-type*."

I brought my magazine over to where Iris was and sat down beside her. I watched as she wrote the word *daguerreotype* over and over until the floor was filled with *daguerreotype*s.

It was after one o'clock when we both got ready for bed. I wondered how much she had accomplished.

She shrugged. "I still think it impossible."

"But you're trying, and that is the main thing."

We got into bed and Iris turned to me. "Bob, you love me?"

"Of course I do," I said, looking into her eyes.

"Then hold me?" she asked.

I held her as she cried herself to sleep. I didn't have to ask why. "Don't worry, you're going to do okay in school. Don't worry," I promised.

There was no response, just the muffled sound of her unhappiness.

CHAPTER THIRTY-NINE
The Hunt

When Saturday arrived, we were off to the bird hunt. I borrowed a shotgun for Iris.

"Now, Iris, you know how to work this thing, don't you?" I asked.

Iris took a deep breath, reaching into the air as she answered what appeared to be a superfluous question. "Now, who been in army? Who train with guns, you or me?"

"Okay, okay, just wanted to make sure you don't blow yourself up."

"Just worry about yourself," Iris said. She took the shotgun from my hands and threw it down on the sofa.

I didn't think the Israeli army had given its soldiers training in quail hunting. When Iris dressed in sneakers and a red sweater,

I was sure they hadn't. I put on my camouflage jacket and work boots.

Charles came to pick us up and we were soon off. The truck bounced along the back roads of the desert until we arrived at the spot Charles felt would be most productive. We each took a place behind some brush along a watering hole and waited for the birds to arrive.

Iris stood holding the gun with one hand as she stuck the muzzle into her foot. She looked around once or twice.

"Where are the birds?" she asked.

"You have to wait for the birds to come in for water, it takes a little patience," I explained. "And get the barrel away from your foot. You're going to blow your leg off."

"*Sheket*, Bob, *sheket*." Iris said with a huff. "This very boring. How much longer we have to wait? When they be here?"

It was obvious Iris was no hunter. "Patience, Iris, patience."

From his cover Charles whispered to us to be quiet so we wouldn't scare the birds away. Iris amused herself by kicking some dirt around. Finally, two birds came flying in. Charles pointed them out and we all raised our guns to shoot. Iris held her shotgun as if it were an Uzi machine gun. The stock was left hanging in the air instead of against her shoulder. I turned in time to stop her from firing.

"Iris, you don't shoot a shotgun like that."

"This is the way I learn in army. You know nothing. This the way I learn."

Oh, God, I thought to myself. She's going to kill herself. "Iris, that's the way you hold an Uzi, but not a shotgun. Now don't fire that thing," I yelled.

Iris raised her voice and pointed her finger at my face. "Now, don't you tell me."

"You two are scaring all the birds away. Be quiet," Charles whispered.

I tried to explain to Iris. "I'm telling you; you're doing it all wrong. The kickback from that gun is going to throw it right out of your hands. I thought you learned all of this in the army. How many times did you fire a gun?"

Iris raised her voice to prove her point. "I shoot it more than you shoot." Then she lowered her voice. "I shoot it twice."

"Twice?" I said, starting to laugh. "That was your total training? Twice?"

Iris was quick to defend herself. "How many times you shoot in army?"

"Never," I responded. "But I know enough to know this is not the way to shoot a shotgun. You can't hold it out in front of you like that. You have to put the stock against your shoulder to absorb the recoil. By the way, did you hit anything in your two shots?"

"I not know, thirty people use the same target. I not able to find my bullet."

"And this, this was your great training in arms. It's good the enemy didn't know about this," I said, continuing to laugh.

Her face became red, her voice rising. "You not make fun of my army. You understand? It best army in the world. You understand? You who never risk anything."

I stopped laughing, seeing how serious she was, and got back to the main topic. "I'm not laughing at you or your army, but two shots at a target full of holes hardly makes you an expert."

Iris turned and started to walk back to the truck. "This is boring. Let's go home."

"Let her go, we can have some quiet. If you two haven't scared all the quail within a hundred miles, we still may get some," Charles said. He waved his hand toward the truck as if to push Iris along.

We had been hunting for only twenty minutes. I didn't want to prove Charles correct in his assessment of women and hunting. "Iris, wait, don't go! You need to be more patient."

I chased after her, noticing she was dragging the butt of the gun along the ground. "Take the bullets out of your gun, or it can go off." As I watched, she dropped the gun to the ground and kept walking. "What the hell are you doing?" I said as I picked the gun up and emptied the chambers.

"This is boring. I not going to just sit there, it a waste of time, nothing happening." Iris said

I was losing patience. "Now, we are not going home. You can sit in the truck, but we ain't leaving."

She climbed into the truck and slammed the door. Through the open window I could hear her say, "I wait here for you and Charles. Hurry up."

I gave another attempt. "Iris, come and try. Just a few more minutes. You haven't even taken a shot yet."

"No, no. You yell at me. You never yell at me again," she said, placing her head against the truck door.

I was determined not to give in to her. I marched back to the watering hole and took cover again behind some tumbleweed. I stood waiting and watching for the birds to return. As dusk approached, several birds came to the water. Charles would shoot once or twice, and feathers would fly. I would unload all five shots in my gun, whose only effect was to provide air-conditioning to any birds in the vicinity. We hunted for forty-five minutes more, until it was dark. I had gone through a box of shells and hit only one bird, and it probably died from laughter.

Charles and I started to walk back to the truck.

"Bob, I told you that to take the little woman out to hunt was a mistake. This is something for men. I would never let Mary hunt. I told you and you didn't listen, so this is what you get," Charles said as he placed his hand on my shoulder. "I hope you've learned your lesson." He grinned and spat some tobacco juice.

"Look, she's my wife. I've got to listen to her sometimes. She thought she could hunt, and she wanted to be with me. What's so terrible?"

"It's just no place for women. You're getting walked over. I told you the bible says the man is head of the house. You can't be a man and let the woman dominate you," Charles said as we neared the truck. He finished with his parting salvo. "I guess you Yankees just don't learn."

Iris opened the door of the truck as we approached. "Well, how many you get?"

"Not too many," I replied.

"How many, not many?"

"Well, I got one bird," I said quietly.

"He ain't much of a hunter," Charles said, spitting more tobacco juice.

Now it was Iris who was laughing. "You mean you do all that shooting for one bird? How many shots you fire?"

"Oh, maybe thirty," I said in a hushed voice.

Iris sat straight up in the cab. "And you say I not know how to shoot. Thirty times you shoot for one bird?" She was half laughing and half yelling. I felt she was really enjoying this interrogation. "That ridiculous! You not come again unless you get to be better shot. You waste money. We could buy birds for what you shoot."

I liked Iris better when she was sulking, but she did have a point. "Well, that's nice coming from you. I stand out there trying to get dinner for my wife and you sit here sleeping."

"Oh, don't be jerk. Get in and let's go home."

Well, I wasn't much of a hunter, and neither was Iris. So what? We had some laughs at each other's expense. This is what being together is all about. How much quail we brought home wasn't important. No, Charles is wrong. Sharing experiences with the one you love is more important than hitting a bird.

CHAPTER FOURTY
Visitors Arrive

The doorbell rang. It was the mail carrier with a package.

Iris called out from the bedroom. "What you get in the mail?"

I was taken by surprise, as I thought she was still sleeping. "Ah, ah, it's a book. Nothing important," I said, going into the bathroom to open my prize.

"You always go into the bathroom to open your mail? I think you lie to me. Come here and show me," she demanded.

Embarrassed, I went to the bedroom, holding the box in one hand, a Civil War pistol in the other.

Iris looked at my prize while loudly stating, "That, that is what you got? That piece of junk? You spend money on that?"

I tried vainly to defend myself. "Yes, I spent money on that. It's a Civil War revolver, a hundred years old, an antique."

Iris laughed. "I think it a piece of junk. In Israel something a hundred years old we dust it off and use it again. This piece of metal not work. It worth nothing. But, most important you lied to me, you tell me it book. This don't look like book to me." She stopped laughing, becoming angry. "You lie to me. That worse thing. How can we be married if you not tell me truth? You try to cover up. That hurt me."

She turned away, ignoring me and starting to get dressed.

"But Iris, I didn't think you'd understand. I know how you hate history, so I didn't mention it."

Iris was on fire. "That's just it. I no understand or you feel that I no understand, then we not able to live together."

I tried to laugh it off. "Now, don't be so serious about this. It's just an old gun, no big deal."

Iris shook her head. "It very important. I sorry you not able to see that. It not what you buy important but that you hide it. This no way to stay together if you lie to me."

I found myself looking at my purchase. Somehow, it didn't seem as great a trophy as it had a few minutes ago. I threw it into the closet.

What next? What other disagreements would we have? Now that her parents are arriving, she will surely return to Israel with them.

* * *

We went to the airport for the arrival of Sarah and Ziggy. Iris was elated to see her parents; I was apprehensive, as they would surely convince her to return to Israel. I welcomed them to Odessa as Iris gave them hugs and kisses. Ziggy and I shook hands.

We all started for the baggage claim. For a minute I felt like I was with the wrong family. Iris and her parents went ahead talking in their native language while I trailed behind. I ran to catch up with the fading backs.

"Did you have a pleasant flight?" I asked as I approached within hearing range. They stopped and turned around as if surprised.

"Oh, Bob. Yes, we had a very pleasant trip," Sarah answered.

"Bob, Bob it good we here. How you say?" Ziggy turned to Sarah for help with his English.

"Yes, you said it right," I interjected.

We stopped at baggage claim to retrieve the luggage. Sarah, Ziggy, and Iris walked on, speaking in Hebrew.

Oh well, they haven't been together for so long and this is their daughter. I guess it is more important that they communicate than I understand.

We arrived back at the apartment. To cut down on costs, Sarah and Ziggy were staying with us. I tried to make Iris's parents feel at home. That is, as comfortable as one could feel when they had the floor for a bed.

Iris and her parents talked among themselves for an hour before her parents turned in, tired from their long trip.

I was in the bedroom when Iris entered. "How are your parents? I heard you all talking like long-lost souls. What were you all chatting about?"

"Oh, I so happy to see my parents. They tell me about Alina and Noah and my friends. They bring pictures of Noah. Noah growing so big, and Alina have boyfriends. I can't wait to go back and see them." Iris was beaming.

The next evening, I arrived home after work. Before dinner, Iris and Sarah went to the kitchen, leaving me and Ziggy alone.

"Well, how do you like the US?" I said as Ziggy and I sat in the living room.

"It good, very good. I here before, ah, ah, how you say..." Ziggy yelled to Sarah in Hebrew for help before continuing: "In summer four years ago we in States. Take car around." Ziggy made a circle with his hands. "We drive in east all around. Go with Lillie and Karel. Oh, very nice, very nice."

It was difficult to make any but the most superficial conversation with Ziggy. To make himself understood by me, each half sentence he would stop to ask Sarah in Hebrew for the equivalent word in English. In the kitchen, separated by a wall from the living room, Sarah was taking charge. I could hear her pulling assorted items from the shelves while giving orders to Iris. Sarah peeked around the wall and peered into the living room.

"Bob, Ziggy, what would you like to eat? I don't know what Iris and I can make, but we will try from what you have here."

I could hear the doors of the refrigerator bang open and closed in the background. The cupboard, as if not to be forgotten, was also joining in the concert.

When all the banging was over, the women had made chicken schnitzel for dinner. Sarah and Iris set the table, and we gathered for our first meal together in the United States.

Before I even sat down, the other three were in deep conversation in their native language. Laughs and shouting, smiling and stares crossed the table as I tried to follow the flow like one trying to steer a boat without a paddle or rudder. I finished my dinner before the others had gotten through the salad. Since I had nothing to contribute to the conversation, my mouth was free for the sole purpose of eating.

I wished I could understand what they were saying. I wished they could understand what I was thinking. *Was this going to solve our marital problems? Why was I being left out of the conversation?*

I got up and turned on the TV. It was most disconcerting to note that no one took the slightest notice. When they finished eating, the table was cleared, and Sarah and Ziggy prepared for bed.

"Will we disturb you if we try to sleep?" Sarah asked as she and Ziggy stretched out on the floor.

"Oh, no. I'm just going to sleep myself. I'll shut the TV off. Good night," I said, wondering whether it was me or the TV they noticed.

I climbed into bed. Iris was already sleeping. She did not even wait for me to hold her. I couldn't help but think I was about as needed as the leftover chicken.

CHAPTER FOURTY-ONE
Small Steps Forward

*B*eing the travel coordinator, I had to come up with something we could do together with Iris's parents. We planned a trip to the mountains of New Mexico to spend a weekend at Dr. Sheets's condo. In the interim I prepared for work each day stepping over, and occasionally on, the floor visitors. The nights continued to be filled with the sound of a foreign language. I should have been content to let this family catch up on all that had happened in the States and Israel.

But wasn't I part of this family now as well? Why don't they include me?

I got up suddenly in the middle of dinner one evening and went to the clinic.

I didn't have anything to do there, so then I just drove around Odessa. I could picture Iris and her parents at the apartment eating and talking. They looked so happy together. Iris just didn't belong in the States. She had never been so happy recently as she was to see her parents. Not this happy when she stepped off the plane from Israel, and certainly not this happy since.

What is left for me to do? I can see that in a short time, I will be a bachelor again. Is it my fault? Could I be doing more to make her happy?

* * *

It was difficult for me to come home from work each evening to a foreign household. Not knowing what anyone else was saying was making me paranoid. When Sarah and Ziggy announced they were going to New Orleans for a few days and then coming back to Odessa, I could hardly restrain myself from packing their suitcases. Now Iris and I could go back to being ourselves.

We drove them to the airport and wished them a pleasant trip.

Finally alone, we were back to our normal routine. Iris had taken a few days off from her classes to be with her parents, and now, in November 1980, was back at school. I felt better coming home from work knowing I had someone to talk to in a language I could understand.

"Iris, there is something I must ask you that has bothered me for the last few days. Why is it that all the time, even while at dinner, you and your parents always spoke in Hebrew? You know I don't understand a word of it. Didn't you realize I would be sitting there, not having the slightest idea what you were saying?"

Iris just went on with her dinner. "Maybe I not want you to understand," she said without emotion, not bothering to look up.

"Hell, that's not very nice to have me sit in my own house eating by myself while you and your parents go on with talking and carrying on, leaving me out. What's the matter with you? I don't want you to do that again. If you want to talk in secret, do it when I'm not around." I raised my voice until I thought passing planes could hear. Turning my back, I went to the bedroom and stretched out on the bed, thinking how wronged I had been.

Iris came in, put her arms around me, and whispered in my ear: "I sorry. It no happen again. You right, it wrong thing to do."

She was as good as her word. When her parents returned to Odessa from New Orleans, there was a lot of broken English but little fluent Hebrew. Although as much as I tried, I couldn't seem to penetrate their family circle. Iris and her mother spent most of the time talking and laughing, more like old high-school friends than mother and daughter. Ziggy would usually come into the tail of the conversation, adding a line or two in a booming voice and placing his arms around his wife and daughter. One didn't have to speak Hebrew to know much love was transpiring between all of them.

* * *

It was almost time for Sarah and Ziggy to return to Israel. I still didn't know if Iris would go with them. A day before the parents were to leave, I confronted Iris. "What did you and your parents talk about?"

"Oh, nothing much. My mother tell me not to be so upset. That marriage is hard and not to be angry with you about cooking and cleaning. That it really a small thing and you will get over it. She tell me you good husband with some bad faults and not to give up."

"Bad faults? Bad faults?" I wrinkled my forehead in mock dejection. "What bad faults?"

"She say you demand too much. That I will learn and that you should calm down and not ask for so much. She tell me not to give up on you."

"Well, I guess that means that you're not going back with them," I said, relieved.

She put her arms around me and whispered in my ear: "Why would I leave the one I love? But you better get rid of bad faults."

Iris was staying, at least for the present.

The next day we took Sarah and Ziggy to the airport and saw them off.

CHAPTER FOURTY-TWO
Success at School

It was the end of November 1980. I was becoming busier at the office. Increasingly satisfied patients returned to me and were referring their friends. I had been in Odessa for almost two years. How long would we remain in Odessa? We had no other immediate choice; we would stay for the present.

One evening as we sat down for a wonderful meal of chicken schnitzel, she told me about a new friend at school. "She very nice, I think I have her come over here if it okay with you."

"Yeah, sure it's okay. This is your house too," I said.

"Oh, Bob, I must tell you what happen in school today. You never believe it. I speak with some people and person ask me where I from 'cause I speak funny. I tell them I from Israel. You not believe what they say to me." Iris paused.

"You're right. I'll never know unless you tell me," I said, starting on the salad.

"Bob, pay attention and listen," she said, putting her hands on her hips. "They want to know if Israel near Dallas. I no believe they so stupid. How they live to get to college and not know Israel a country?"

I started to laugh.

"It not funny—it sad," Iris replied.

I was still smiling. "What's really sad is not that they didn't know where Israel is but that they mistook your accent for a Texas drawl. Now that's dumb." I changed the subject. "Hey, this dinner is good. You never made chicken schnitzel before. Where did you get the recipe?"

"My mother give it to me. She leave me many good ideas," Iris said, smiling.

I could hardly believe she had made the meal. As I stuffed my mouth I was soon brought back to reality.

"When you done, you do dishes," Iris commanded.

"I have work to do. I've got my reading and a new surgical procedure that I must study."

Iris went to the bedroom to retrieve her schoolbooks. On returning she said, "Well, that mean you got to do dishes tomorrow or whenever you find the time."

ROBERT JAFFEE, MD

I got up and started clearing the table. *Damn it, damn it,* I said to myself as I removed the remaining dishes to the sink. Turning to Iris, I expressed my displeasure.

"When are you going to do all the things a housewife is supposed to do?"

Iris made herself comfortable and started opening one of her books. "Never. You want dog, not wife. I not dog. Now, shut up so I can study," she said calmly.

I don't believe this. I must shut up and do the dishes so she can study?

I started to smile. It began to dawn on me that maybe Iris was correct. I didn't want a doormat as a wife. She was showing the qualities that first drew her to me. She went by her own mind. I had to earn her love and respect, not demand it. This made her love even more valuable.

I was glad Iris was standing up for what she thought was right. She was not going to be bullied by me. I was starting to realize that being a husband was more than just bringing home a paycheck.

I finished the dishes and started my medical reading. I read for about a half hour while Iris filled up several pages that quickly passed to the floor. When I looked up, she was surrounded by valleys and mountains of paper.

"What are you trying to do, ruin all the forests of the world?" I asked.

"No, this really boring. I never learn English. It no make sense," she said, slapping shut one of her books. "I think I go develop film now. We learn how to in class. I able to do negatives here and do prints at school. Tonight, I see if I able to develop at home. I buy everything. I hope it work."

This was news to me. "Where are you going to do it?"

"In the bathroom. I need someplace dark to work," she said, going off to gather her materials. She went out to the car and returned with several gallons of chemicals as well as developing tanks, reels, film, and her camera.

"Why don't you carry one piece at a time?"

She screamed back, "What the hell you sit there for? Come and help me."

I got up and grabbed some of the things before she dropped them and "developed" the rug. After putting all the equipment in the bathroom without incident, I went back to studying, while Iris started to read the directions to mix the chemicals. Five minutes passed with the rustling of glass and banging of closet doors before she proclaimed that she wasn't able to continue.

Iris looked like a woman within a bottle as she stood encircled by every piece of glassware we owned. With a huff of resignation, she proclaimed that she could not find the right bottles to mix the chemicals in. I went over to read the labels on the chemicals and soon had the proper mixtures put together. It was mostly a problem with pints and quarts, since Iris was familiar with the metric rather than English system.

Solitude and harmony returned as Iris, armed with the proper mixtures, was ready to develop film.

She placed a kiss on my lips as my reward for being so smart.

There was no use in my being modest. "You're so fortunate to have such a brilliant, good-looking, kind husband. I'm simply perfect, I guess." Even to me this sounded like a bit much as I choked out the last few words.

"You're not bad to begin with. I think you smart, only you terrible lover. If you think you perfect in bed—"

I cut her off before she started giving proof of her allegations. "Okay, okay, I get the point. Go develop pictures," I said, smiling.

With the crisis over, it was back to my reading. Settling in my chair, I picked up a medical journal. As I read the first few paragraphs, the lights went out.

"Bob, I need complete darkness when I take the film out of camera," Iris called from the bathroom.

"What the hell are you doing? I can't work in the dark. Put those lights back on!"

"No, no, you'll ruin everything. Leave the lights off."

"Hurry up," I yelled back. "Forget about my studying, but I'm going to kill myself walking into things if you don't hurry." I stood up, afraid to move, clutching my magazine as if it were my link to sanity. Finally, the lights came back on.

Iris came out of the bathroom. "Hey, what you think I here for? You doctor and I only in college, but this as important to me as your work to you. I need time to do my work. You have to understand that I person," she said holding her small developing tank like a hand grenade she was about to throw.

I quietly went back to my reading as Iris continued developing her film. As she was finishing, I got up to admire the hanging strip of negatives dripping dry from their last rinse. "You know, they really look good. I'm proud of you," I said, kissing her on the cheek. "They're terrific."

We went to bed and I held her as she cried softly until falling asleep.

I was starting to be a husband, slowly, but at least making a beginning.

* * *

Iris was busy, dividing her time between school, home, and teaching at the Hebrew school.

It was a sunny Saturday morning in December 1980 when Iris brought up her teaching.

"Bob. If they no want to learn, I not teach them. These children want to play. It okay with me—I not waste my time," Iris said on returning from the Hebrew school. "Maybe I make game out of learning. I hold up picture of vegetable and ask them to name it. What you think of idea?" she asked, falling onto the sofa.

"I thought you didn't care whether they learned or not," I answered.

"Well, I try one more thing. If this not work, then I give up. But I do that later. Now it time for me to go out with friend to take pictures. She be here soon," she said as she got up and went into the bedroom to change her teaching clothes to jeans and T-shirt for her outing.

I watched her rush around gathering her camera, extra lenses, and film. "Who are you going with?" I asked, aiming my questions as best I could at the moving target.

"Oh, my friend Rosie. She my best friend at school. We sit together. She from Mexico. We get along very well. She take me yesterday for piña colada. You know, Bob, I like piña colada. It make me a little drunk, but it really good."

I turned my head to one shoulder and raised my eyebrows. "What type of education are you getting? I don't want you to be an alcoholic. What are you doing, drinking piña coladas for lunch? What kind of friend do you have?"

Iris continued to dress and gather her equipment. "Now, don't get excited. I just have one. I never have one before. We just thirsty, and you can get them in little cans to drink, cold too."

I closed in on Iris, pointing my finger at her. "You listen to me. That is something that is not good for you. Believe me, you can live without alcohol for lunch. Don't get started on a bad habit. Who is this friend anyway? I don't want you going out with people like that. Now I tell—"

Iris returned to the living room looking like she was ready for a safari. "Quiet down! I not little girl." She came up to me where I was sitting on the couch. "Now give me kiss," she demanded as the doorbell rang.

I pulled back and smiled. "I am not going to kiss a future drunk."

"Oh, Bob, you idiot. But I love you anyway, so I give you kiss." She kissed my cheek and went to answer the door.

The woman who came through the door was about Iris's age though much shorter. The two were like opposites: blond, thin Iris with her freckled skin and Rosie with her tan complexion, dark hair and medium build. "Glad to meet you," said Rosie in greeting. "Iris has told me so much about you, or as she says, 'Bub.' We have so much fun with her accent. Everybody thinks it is so cute—we all laugh, and so does Iris. She is really the hit of the class. There really isn't anyone like her."

Iris took Rosie's hand and led her out the door, calling back to me: "I be back to make dinner, don't you worry," and they were gone.

I sat down to read, but the "excitement" of the medical journals soon had me asleep. It wasn't until four thirty that I was awakened by Iris's footsteps. I at once straightened as if I had read for long, hard hours.

"Bob, Rosie and I get some very nice pictures but it not enough. If not getting late and time to make dinner I would stay longer," Iris said bursting through the door and kissing me. "What you do today?" she asked.

"Oh, just reading, that's all, just reading," I said, leaving out the nap.

"Bob, you soon know everything. I got to make dinner. You want to help?" she asked.

"Do I have to?"

"No, it okay, you get dishes again. And I no want to hear complaint," Iris called from the kitchen. To the accompaniment of banging pans, she made a delicious dinner of her new favorite and maybe only dish, chicken schnitzel.

For me, there was no use getting angry. The cleanup was mine. Besides, I had decided to give this sharing thing a chance. But I didn't have to like it. I ground my teeth and clenched my fists and felt my face flush as I did the dishes.

After dinner and cleanup, Iris went back to her homework.

"This English impossible, but teacher say I doing better. I think maybe I able to do it, but it take forever. Why it so hard?" she said, tossing another page to the floor.

I could see she was making definite progress as she had graduated to two English words vying for space on a paper. Iris compared her written words with the printed version. A smile came over her face; it was correct.

CHAPTER FOURTY-THREE
Understanding

*I*ris would come by the office or call each day at about 5:00 p.m. After dealing with people between the ages of sixty and eighty all day, the appearance of someone under thirty made me look twice to make sure it wasn't a mirage. Iris coming down the hall with her hair flowing out behind her, looking for her Bob, was a pleasant sight to see, but on this day it still annoyed me. Maybe because I felt that an office is for work and spouses should keep out. Maybe I felt that she came to check on me. I don't know.

"Where's Bob?" I heard Iris ask Libby.

"He's seeing a patient. I'll tell him you're here," Libby responded.

I finished the patient's exam and came out to greet my wife. No matter how many times she came to see me at the office, she always had that twinkle in her eyes, that excitement, as if it was her first visit. I was behind in my patient schedule and was rushing to catch up.

"What's up?" I asked Iris hurriedly.

"Nothing, I just come to visit husband. When you home?" she asked.

I took her to a private corner. "Look Iris, I'm really busy."

"What you mean, you too busy to spare a second for wife? I go."

The sparkle in her eyes was gone as she turned to leave, and she looked down at her feet as she started to walk away. Oh, hell, I thought. I don't want her to be angry. I caught up to her and reached out for her shoulder. "I didn't say I didn't want you here. I'd much rather be with you than a bunch of complaining patients. It's just that I'm busy."

Iris turned around and shot back. "You always busy." Then she calmed down, giving me a chance to redeem myself. "Kiss me."

"Where, here in the office?" I answered surprised.

"Why not? Don't you love me in the office as well as at home? You think I different woman in different places?" She kissed me on the lips, turned away, and then suddenly remembered why she had come. "Bob, you be home at six, 'cause that when dinner be ready. Bye." And she was gone.

Arriving home that evening, I marveled that the same woman who couldn't heat a can of corn six months ago was making delicious meals.

"Bob, my mother and Lillie give me some nice recipes, see here," she said shoving a small box toward me.

I investigated the wooden box, which held cards arranged alphabetically. "Iris, how can you write the cards in Hebrew and arrange them according to an English alphabet?"

As she finished setting the table she nonchalantly answered: "It because Israelis very smart. Now come and eat before it get cold. I have to talk to you."

I eagerly sat down as Iris continued. "I must tell you how much I like photography. I think my teacher very good. He say that all these pictures of setting suns just junk. Really, there no imagination in those pictures, they boring," Iris said, grabbing my hand and preventing me from eating.

"Iris, that's nice. I'm glad that after three months you're an expert on photography. You're also letting the food get cold while you hold me," I said, looking toward my captive arm.

"Now, Bob, you no make fun of me. I take some nice pictures. Wait, I go show them to you." She ran off to retrieve her photographs.

I took the opportunity to shovel as much food into my mouth as possible, chicken marsala, asparagus, mashed potatoes. Iris returned thrusting her album beneath my eyes. Her enthusiasm and pride were evident across the table. I had a mouthful of food and inadvertently coughed up a little onto her pictures. Suddenly, her facial expression changed. The smile on her face was gone as she reached for her photos.

"What you do?" She ripped the photos away from me. "You no care, you dirty my pictures. You not interested in anything I do. How you love me if you not care what I do?" She gently stroked the food from the photos. Glistening tears formed in her eyes.

I attempted a defense. "Iris, I'm eating. This is not the time to show me pictures."

She jumped on my words like a bird of prey on a mouse. "Oh, you always have some excuse. It either work or a meeting, but it always something. You just not care what I do."

I reached over to her, but she pulled away, grasping her album as if it was the only object that supported her.

I put down my fork and looked up at her. "Listen, just listen, you don't have to look at me but listen. I love you. I love you very much. It's true that I don't know about photography, but it's not true that I don't care about what you do. I want you to succeed at what you do, to be the best. That is what marriage is about. Whether your pictures are good or bad, I can't judge, but the enthusiasm that you have and the pleasure you derive is something I want to help grow. I want you to have the surroundings and the environment to accomplish whatever dreams you have."

She just stood there. I could see I had her attention, because she stopped cleaning her photos and didn't move. I continued: "As people we may not show our emotions in the same way. You're more expressive in your love. You like to kiss and hug. Those are good things, but what can I say? I was brought up to be more reserved, to hide my feelings. If I don't kiss you ten times a day, it isn't because I don't care. I hope you will feel my sincerity in the way I look at you, in the way I hold you, even if it is only once a day. But enough talk: words will never replace the feeling I get when I hold somebody I really care for. For me, that person is you. Now allow me to hold you."

She turned and threw her arms around me. "Bob, you understand a lot."

I wasn't returning the love she showered on me. I was too concerned with myself and not giving her the time she needed from me—nor was I showing the feelings I had for her. If I had to explain my love because she didn't feel it, then something was wrong with me. She knew how to express herself, and I didn't.

No, it is you, Iris, who understands a lot.

CHAPTER FOURTY-FOUR
Adapting

*I*ris, since it will soon be Christmas, it's necessary that we buy some gifts for the people I work with most closely, office presents," I said.

Iris was perplexed. "Why, you have to buy them presents? You not Catholic, you not even their boss. Leave it to Dr. Sheets to give presents."

"I can't do that. First of all, it's the custom to give presents at the year's end, even if I'm not their religion. Besides, do you want them to call me a cheap Jew?"

Iris shook her head. "It sound stupid to me. You all the time complain about money and now you want to give presents."

"Don't be cheap. You sound like me. These people work hard, they don't earn very much—"

"So how that your problem? You on salary too," Iris said.

"Yeah, but my salary is a lot more than theirs. Maybe we could call them Hanukah presents."

This brought a smile to her lips. "Very funny, very funny. Then no one know what gifts are for. It like different country to me. I not used to everything being Christmas. In Israel stores not make such big thing over it."

"But you're not in Israel. You're in the US, and Jews are the minority here."

Iris curled up on the sofa to do some homework. I could tell she was making progress in her English by the decreased number of papers that hit the floor.

While writing she commented: "My English teacher give me B in last paper. She says I get much better. I wish she let me write homework in Hebrew—it be much easier for me."

Laughing, I walked over to the sofa. "Then it wouldn't be English. Be grateful they're not making you take math." I reached for one of her papers. "Hey, this looks pretty good," I said as I read part of her composition. Gone was the repetition of one word. There were now pages filled with complete sentences and paragraphs. I bent over and kissed her on the cheek. "I'm proud of you, I really am. This is good."

"What, you think I dumb? Now you see, if I can learn English, then you can learn Hebrew."

"Wait a minute," I said, putting her papers down. "Maybe you're not dumb, but I'm afraid I am."

"Bob, you be sorry when children speak Hebrew and you not able to talk to them. Anyhow, I do this later. Time for me to go to school and develop pictures."

I looked at my watch. "It's seven o'clock at night. Where are you going?"

"The school open the lab till nine o'clock. My friend Rosie is in charge. We have lots of fun joking around. I even get some work done. She very nice. She even like to smoke pot."

I was stunned. "What, what, you smoke pot! What's going on? I'm sending you to school. I thought—"

Applying her makeup without pausing, she quietly responded: "Oh Bob, you old. You ever try it?"

"Once or twice," I said softly, trying to hide my lack of experience.

Iris closed her lipstick and put it back into her purse. "How you talk if you not know? You should try it, much better for sex."

"What? You take it before sex? How did you get so much experience? Where did you get so much expertise in this? I'm married to a drug addict and sex maniac," I said in mocking admonishment.

"Oh, don't get so upset what you not know anything about," she advised me, grabbing her film and heading for the door.

I followed her to the car. "What do you mean, I don't know anything about it? You talking about drugs or sex?"

As she started up the car, she put her head out the window, turned toward me smiling. "Both! Bye, be back later."

I smiled to myself as I returned to the apartment. Iris was becoming independent. She was developing a life of her own. She had made some friends: Carmella, Curtis, and now Rosie. She was improving her English and finding an interest in photography.

Maybe she could find lasting happiness here, with me.

CHAPTER FORTY-FIVE
A Week Away

It was January 1982. I had put aside a few days to take a medical course in New York City. Iris would remain in Odessa. Having made some friends, I didn't feel she would be alone.

She lay on the bed pretending to be asleep, sneaking looks at me while I packed.

"Now, Bob, you call me every day. You promise?" she said, sitting up. Her soft voice sounded dejected.

I continued to gather clothes for my suitcase. "Iris, where are my brown pants? I know they're here somewhere," I said, looking in the closet.

Iris got up and stood behind me. "You no hear what I say. Now listen. It very important that you call me every day. Now tell me you no forget." She put her arms around my neck and planted a kiss to my lips.

Finding my brown pants, I turned, staring into her eyes. I never appreciated how blue they were, so beautiful. "Now, you promise?" she cooed.

I wrapped my arms and the brown pants around her neck. "I love you, but do we have to make the phone company rich with our love?"

Iris shook her head. She moved her hair away from her face. "No, I not care. You call every day." She relaxed her tone. "I love you very much. I want to hear you every day and know what you do and that you okay. Now, you promise?"

She kept her arms around me and the brown pants. "Yes, okay, I promise. But I think you'd better let go of me before the pants need to be ironed."

As I went back to packing, I glimpsed Iris's finger shaking at me. "You not forget, you promised. Now, you remember."

That evening I arrived in New York City. Alone in the hotel room, I didn't find much to do except watch TV. As I was about to doze off, I remembered to call Iris. Her voice sounded so distant, and she spoke in a monotone. I asked if anything was wrong. In the background I could hear voices.

"Bob, I miss you. When you be home?"

I let out a deep breath of relief. "Is that all, Iris? I thought something serious was wrong. I'm glad to hear you're not hurt."

"I not all right. I miss you."

"I miss you too. But I'll be back soon. I am going to see my parents and Steven and Lillie after the course. Who are those voices in the background?"

"That my friend and her boyfriend. They come over. Bob, come home sooner. I need you."

"Don't be like that. You know I want to see my folks. You have your friends there. It's only a week; you're not alone. Do you need anything?"

There was just silence, but hearing the voices in the background, I knew the line was still connected. Finally, after about thirty seconds she said very faintly, "What you say?"

I pressed the phone closer to my ear. "I'll call you tomorrow, okay?"

Again, a long silence. "You come home. I need you."

I repeated that I wasn't going to return early and terminated the call. I couldn't understand what she was so upset over. She had to learn that she could survive for a few days without me. She wasn't in any physical emergency and had friends with her. I was sorry she was lonely, but she had to learn that I might be away for courses, and she would be alone for short periods.

Perhaps I should have taken her along, but it was too late to change anything.

After three days the course in Manhattan ended. I rented a car and drove the short distance to Queens to see my parents.

My parents had grown up during the Depression. My mother lost her home as a child when her parents couldn't pay the mortgage. My father had had to wait seven years to complete his degree in dentistry because he could not pay the tuition. They had imparted upon me not only the importance of having and saving money, but how fickle life can be.

It was reassuring to go back home, like a plane returning to Earth. I slept in my room, that I had shared with my younger brother. Our house was small for the five people that lived there growing up, my parents, older and younger brother. Three male children, a father and one mother shared one bathroom. It was bedlam in the mornings when everybody screamed to use the bathroom. As I slept in my old bed I reached over to a drawer in the adjoining desk. There I went through some of the belongings I had stored there reminiscing over how I had obtained them and enjoying the memories. A civil war bullet reminded me of how my father had taken me to the Gettysburg battlefield as a young child. When I got that bullet, I slept with it under my pillow. Many mornings I would look at it wondering who had dropped it, had he survived the war? Also in the draw was a letter from my medical school (The Medical College of Wisconsin) informing me that I was alternate thirteen on their acceptance list. They had taken eleven alternates the year before. I was accepted two weeks before school started, probably the last person to get in. I smiled to myself as I graduated in the top ten percent of my class with honors. With a smile on my face and a bullet in my palm I fell asleep.

* * *

My next stop was a stay at Steven's and Nancy's house in Monticello, a two-hour drive. The town, in the two years since I left, hadn't changed: a core of desolation surrounded by beautiful mountains.

I got together with Steven, Nancy, Karel, and Lillie for dinner one evening. While the rest ate in the dining room, I slipped into the kitchen, sat down, and called Iris. She was quiet, hardly saying anything. She again pleaded for me to return.

In frustration I slapped my hand on my lap and then placed it over my eyes. "Iris, I have only two more days here and then I'll be home. What is the emergency? You have your friends there, and you have money. Are you sick or something?" I asked.

There was no response. I kept asking if she was still on the line. Steven, in the next room, could overhear the conversation and the silent pauses. "How can they have a marriage if they can't even talk to each other?" I heard him say loudly.

Wishing I had some privacy, I put down the silent receiver long enough to tell the dining-room crowd to be quiet.

After a long pause Iris said limply, "Bob, I need you. I love you very much."

From the depth of her emotion, I felt like a soldier off to war or a condemned man going to his execution rather than a husband away for week from his wife. What the hell was going on? I didn't know whether to be flattered or irate at such commotion over so trivial an experience. She entreated me to stay on the phone and talk, but I was at Steven's place, and he started yelling in the background about the cost.

"Iris, I can't talk forever. I've got to go," I explained.

She begged me to talk longer, but I had to end the call, telling her I would return soon, and I would call again tomorrow. I of course told her I loved her too. There were only two days remaining.

* * *

It was no surprise that a big kiss and hug greeted me at the airport on my arrival back in Odessa. I had only been gone a week, but from her reaction I sensed it seemed much longer for Iris.

"Here, I carry your stuff," Iris said. "No, I change my mind. I kiss you."

"Please, people are going to think I'm being mugged," I told her jokingly as she jumped on me, once again demanding a display of affection. Her arms wrapped around me holding me immobile while she planted kiss after kiss upon my lips.

"Hun, easy, easy its only been a week. People are going to think I've returned from the dead." I mumbled between kisses.

"Bob, you hopeless," she puffed out. "I not know who care that you and I kiss." She dropped her arms and picked up my luggage.

"Give me the luggage, it's heavy." I said, grabbing the handles from her. She then hooked her right arm around my left one and placed her head on my shoulder. We walked out of the airport to the car. It was comforting for me to have my love again at my side. I felt so relieved, like the way one feels when a plane first touches earth on landing. For no reason it suddenly dawned on me. I had a good job and a loving, beautiful, smart wife. I was a lucky man. When we reached the car, she released her hold on me as I placed my bags in the trunk. "How was your trip?"

"It was all right. I learned a lot in my course and enjoyed visiting my parents. Steven, Nancy, Lillie, and Karel all send their regards. How was it here? Did you and your friends have a good time?"

Iris looked away from me. "Oh, it not good. My friend bring her boyfriend with her. While I on the phone with you she and boyfriend sit in living room and kiss. I think they like to come 'cause they have no other place to kiss. It terrible for me. I feel so alone and miss you very much. Bob, you kiss me," she said, looking up into my eyes.

Now I understood why she had been so reticent on the phone. "Of course, I'll kiss you," putting my arms around her, and lifting her up. "I didn't know you had such a bad time of it while I was gone. Why didn't you tell me what was going on when we talked on the phone?"

She leaned her head against my shoulder. "What you do about it in New York?"

"I would have told you to throw them out. Why didn't you get rid of them?"

Iris responded quietly. "I afraid. I all alone and I tell them to leave, but they not go. What I suppose to do?"

I rubbed her back and kissed her cheek. "It's okay now. Let's forget about it and go home."

We entered the car, kissed again and drove home.

* * *

As I unpacked my suitcase that evening, I noticed two of my shirts on the bed rolled up under one of the pillows.

"What are these shirts doing here? Did you run out of your own?" I asked.

"No, I get so alone that I sleep with these. They smell like you so they make me feel that you here." She smiled. "Now I have the real thing, I no need shirts."

She is too important for me to leave alone; she's coming on any future trip I make.

CHAPTER FOURTY-SIX
A Bad Day

As my surgical load increased along with improved results, my confidence and ego grew. I wanted to discuss with Iris how long we should remain in Odessa and when we should consider opening my own practice.

One day, as I read some medical journals at home, waiting for Iris to arrive, I slipped into my usual daydreams of my imaginary new practice with all its prestige and monetary rewards. I looked at my watch, noticing it was already six o'clock. Iris was no doubt busy developing pictures. When finally I heard her footsteps outside, I was relieved. I listened as the steps came closer to the apartment door. The distinct sound had just a little slide to each step, just barely, as if not quite sure of the direction. I went to the door to greet her.

"Oh, Bob," she muffled out between sobs. "You not believe what happen to me, it horrible." She flung herself around me like a tightly wrapped coat, burying her head into my shoulder. Occasionally, a mumble emanated from the hidden, weeping face.

I gently took hold of her head and moved it away from my chest. "Look at me. I can't understand a word you're saying. Take your head away from me for a second."

Taking her head off my shoulder she cleared the tears from her eyes. "They call me a Jew bastard." Unable to say more, she returned to the nest of my shoulder.

"What happened? What did they call you? Stop hiding and say something. I can't understand what you're trying to say." She just continued to be pasted to my breast. I moved back and pushed her away.

"They say I Jew bastard. I no understand why they say something like that. I not want to hurt them. Why they do this to me?"

I still could not believe what I had heard. "Who called you that? Explain a little." She again wiped the tears from her face with her now soaked sleeve and took a few seconds to compose herself.

Between sniffles she went on: "I in class and we discuss about holidays. A lady say that it not fair that all Catholic holidays are not days off from school. I say that Jewish holidays are not holidays from school, so why should Catholic holidays be? She look at me and say that I not know anything 'cause I a Jew bastard. Bob, why they say something like that? I not go back. They call me this and laugh all the time at my accent. They think it funny, and they make fun of me. I make believe I not care but it all hurt, it hurt not to be the same. I not go back." She moved to the other shoulder, using my shirt as a towel to absorb the flood.

"Please, stop crying," I said as I dug her head out of my chest. I had always been afraid this might happen, and now it had. It was so hard to see Iris hurt. "Iris, people who say things like that are idiots."

"But why, why they want to hurt me so much?" she sobbed.

I tried to be philosophical. "It's not you they are trying to hurt; it is their own ignorance that they can't control. Don't get upset. Realize their shortcomings."

"But it hurt. It hurt me so much. I try to keep it in when people make fun of me but it make me cry inside. I don't want people to know that it get to me so I act like it not. I just say I sorry that she feel that way and I hope she change her mind," Iris said as her tears started to recede.

I could not believe this young woman had such composure under these circumstances. "Good, Iris. That is the right thing to say."

"But what good it do? They still think me a bastard."

I held her as I tried to give some wisdom to something that defied explanation. "Iris, what they think is not important. What you think of yourself is. You have accomplished so much in the brief time you've been here. You have taken on challenges those people couldn't tackle in their dreams. How many people could come to a new land and new language and succeed? You've done that."

"If I do that, why they still laugh at me?"

I grasped her tighter and closer as I shook my head and answered: "It is not your fault. There will always be ignorant people needing to get ahead by putting other people down. You can give in to them and fold up and quit when they attack you, or you can forget them and go on with your life, realizing how wrong they are and not letting them get you down."

Iris took a tissue from her purse to dab a latent tear. "But I not able to forget. I not strong enough. I feel so bad inside that—"

I so much wanted to reassure her. "Yes, yes, I know, but you mustn't quit. You have so much you want to accomplish. Don't let their prejudice stop you. In the end you will determine your life, not them. That is, if you don't allow them to cut you down. It's not easy. I told you there was prejudice here, and that eventually it would affect you. This is not Israel, and Jews are the minority here. But most people are not like this lady. Don't judge everyone by this one stupid person." I squeezed her so tightly I was afraid I would crush her. Her hair felt so soft as I stroked it.

Seconds passed, then I felt Iris stroking my head. Her spread-out fingers trickled down my neck, warm as the rain on a hot summer evening.

"I don't know what else to say. There is nothing that will make it better, that will make the pain less," I intoned soothingly. "But what choice do you have? If you give in, then they have succeeded. No, you can't quit." I paused and said softly, "It's easy for me to talk. I only hope you will stay here with me."

Iris pulled back from me as she replied: "I never think it be so hard. I try, but all the time they make fun of me that they laugh at me for the way I talk. I try not to show them it hurt. What can I do to change the way I talk? I not able to help it. I think they never stop to laugh at me."

She put her head back on my shoulder. I was glad she could not see me dry my own eyes. "I don't know what to say. I just don't know what—" I choked, trying to find some words to dissipate the despair, the emptiness she felt; but words were inadequate. There was nothing but silence.

CHAPTER FOURTY-SEVEN
Coming Together

*L*ife picked up for Iris as she made progress in her photography class. I was returning from the office for dinner one evening in February when Iris greeted me with good news.

"My pictures so good that my teacher, Bill, say I one of best in class. He say someday I be real good photographer. Rosie and me go out and take lots of photos. It important to get good pictures."

She was especially happy about a call from Israel. "My parents call me. They want us to go to Israel in March for Passover. What you think? I want to go so much to see my family."

I wasn't sure I could go. I told her I would see if I could take the time off from work. The following evening, I returned to an empty apartment, as Iris was at school developing her photos. I was pleased to find that a new Civil War artifact I ordered had arrived. It didn't appear to be much—a round, rusted piece of iron that had once been a cannonball. To most people, it would look like an oversized and much-abused doorstop, but to me, the history of the flaking iron was immense. Maybe this shot was used at Gettysburg, or perhaps it was in the caisson brought to the front lines at Appomattox and never fired.

Iris walked in. "Bob, you not believe—we going to have show in shopping mall and I going to have several of my pictures there. I so excited." Pausing, she looked at my new acquisition. "Bob, what is this? You really overdo yourself with this," she said, trying to figure out what it was.

She took it from my hands. "Oh, you kidding, this is so heavy." The cannonball dropped to the floor. "Bob, this really silly. Now you say we should save money and you buy junk like this. I ask you to explain this, but I not see any way it make sense. Now you—"

I sat staring at my rusted metal as Iris kicked it.

I felt humiliated. "Enough, I'm tired of listening to your criticism. This piece of junk was only thirty dollars. I work for the money, and this is what I like to buy, it's my hobby. So, you don't understand it—so what? I like it; it makes me happy. Don't you think I'm worth thirty dollars? You want cameras and film. You go through photographic paper like it was as common as a drop of rain in a storm, but if I spend some money on myself—even if it's only a few dollars—you ridicule me." My voice started to break as my emotion increased. "I think it unfair of you, very unfair."

I no longer felt interested in my new possession and just left it to roll around on the floor as I went to the bedroom to lie down. A few seconds later I heard the front door close as Iris left the apartment.

It isn't right of her to make such a fool of me. So, what if she thinks it is stupid? I suppose buying a piece of old rust is a little dumb, but I like it and that's what is important.

I soon fell asleep.

I was awakened by the feeling of something hitting me. My eyes opened to find Iris hanging up her coat. On top of me was a small package. "What's this?"

"Open it. It's for you," Iris answered, returning to the bed.

From inside the bag protruded what looked like a foot. I pulled it out. There was a rag doll with an enormous nose, and across its belly was written "Nobody is Perfect."

I felt an immediate smile chase the look of speculation from my face. I grabbed Iris and kissed her, pulling her close to me and whispering in her ear: "I hope you don't think that looks like me."

"No, I just want to say I wrong, and I see this and it just right. Love is seeing through eyes of a different color. But you know, it not bad likeness."

Now we were both laughing. "That's it. Now I'm going to buy five more cannonballs for that insult."

"Oh, don't you dare. Come on, help me make dinner. I have a lot I want to tell you."

I got up and went out to the kitchen, where she stood over a recipe written in Hebrew, following the directions as she pointed out the items she was to use.

"Give me that, the one marked number three." She ordered, but realizing I couldn't read Hebrew, she pushed me away to get at a spice.

"How do I know that you're not trying to poison husband and become rich American widow?" I jested.

Iris looked up at me. "Ha, you think I marry you if I want to be rich? What you think I get for all that rust metal you have? Most people die and leave money—you leave cannonball. Anyway, Bob, listen. First, I have to hurry to develop pictures so I able to be ready for exhibition. I must get them perfect, and I need money to buy more paper."

I was glad to see her so interested in her work, and readily agreed to finance it further. She was so excited about the exhibition, which was to be held in the shopping center across from our apartment building.

We ate dinner quickly, and she was soon off to the school to do her developing.

That evening Steven called. I told him that I could not start a practice with him as Iris was against it.

He was not happy. "What does she know? She's just a kid. She doesn't even know me. How can she have reservations about us working together? Look, you do what you want. I'm just telling you I can't wait any longer. Enough said.

"How's married life?" he said, changing the subject.

I was happy to tell him that Iris had made tremendous progress. "She's made friends; she cooks; and most of all she really loves me—"

Steven could not resist a jab. "If she loves *you*, then I'd keep her. Finding someone to love *you* is not easy."

"Oh, shut up. Iris has really started to become a great wife. Things are getting better. She doesn't cry as much at night. I think she is really settling in, and her photography is getting quite good. It's remarkable, all the progress she's made. And I've done some adjusting too." I was speaking to myself as much as to Steven. "I've even started to share the housework. Yes, this marriage is working out."

Steven was true to form in his reply. "It's a cinch she didn't marry you for money or looks. Well, since you're not about to commit suicide and you're starting to bore me, I'm going to hang up. Bye."

CHAPTER FOURTY-EIGHT
Good Tears

*B*ob, Bob, oh, you must see these pictures. I think they're wonderful," Iris proudly announced upon her arrival home from school. Before I could respond, her coat was off, and the pictures were in her hands. "See this one: it good, you think?" she asked, handing me a picture of three boys taken from their backs peering into the blank screen of an arcade game.

I looked at the photo. To me it told a story of the void of these faceless people just peering onto a blank screen. "I like it. I really do." Before I could say another word, a multitude of pictures were in my lap.

"See this one, and this one—"

"Wait, wait. One at a time," I said, picking up one of the pictures, while several others slipped from my lap to the floor.

"Oh, be careful, Bob. Watch what you do," Iris said, grabbing the photos and tenderly dusting them off.

I looked intently at each of them. "These are good. I mean it. Why, I didn't know you had such talent." I locked eyes with an eighty-year-old cowboy holding onto the reins of three horses. At one time, the old man likely stood above these animals; only the resolve chiseled into his face remained of the force he probably once was. It was more than a photo; it was a statement about the character of the man and the rugged life he must have lived.

"Bob, in a couple of weeks we have photographer come. He going to choose the best, so I want these to be good. I work very hard on these." Iris then pulled from her portfolio fifteen more photographic prints, all made from the same negative.

To my uneducated artistic eye, they all looked alike. "What the hell is this? How many of these do you have? Are you going to sell them?"

Iris turned toward me and in a condescending tone answered: "See, you know nothing. Here I show you. This one a little too dark, and this one have a piece of dust right here, and this one . . ."

"Okay, okay, I get the point."

She continued: "And because it all need to be so perfect, I need a little more money to buy some paper and to frame them."

I took hold of Iris and kissed her on the forehead. "For such a promising photographer, of course. I am very proud. Now, it's late. Let's get some sleep."

Iris gently eased her photos back into her folder, smiling and humming to herself.

We got into bed, and the topic turned to the upcoming trip to Israel. I had told Iris that I could not get time off from work to go to Israel. I suggested that she go alone in March and stay for a month. I knew she wanted to be with her family for the Jewish holiday of Passover. It would also be one year since she had come to the US.

She was hesitant. "But what you do here alone? I not able to stay for such a long time and leave you here."

"Iris, the costly part of the trip is the airfare. Once you are there, the rest is cheap. You probably have a lot of friends you want to see, some old boyfriends, no doubt, too. All I ask is that you don't fall in love with some general and not come back."

"Oh, I not do that. You really think I go there to see old boyfriends?" she said suddenly sitting up in bed and staring at me. She continued in a softer but still stern tone. "Promise me you go out for Passover, that you not stay by yourself. You can go to the temple. They are having a Passover service. Now, promise me you will go."

"I don't know. You know how I hate those formal things and—"

"You go! I not want you alone. You should be with people. I worry about you if you not go. I not able to have a good time if you here by yourself."

I put my arm around her and whispered: "Don't worry, I'll do my best." She kissed me, and I held her as she began to fall asleep.

For about a month I had missed the soft, muffled crying as the lights went out, but tonight, it returned. "What's the problem?"

She shrugged her shoulders. "I so happy, I go to see family."

"Well, as long as it's for a good cause you can cry," I said, pulling her head into my chest and stroking her hair as I held her. "Good night, Iris. I love you very much."

CHAPTER FOURTY-NINE
Happy at Last

*I*t was the end of February 1982, eleven months since we had married. The weather was becoming warmer in Odessa, not that it stayed cold for very long. I thought Iris might enjoy going to Ruidoso for a weekend while there was still snow in the mountains and maybe go skiing. We could invite Avi and Carmella to join us. I found that Dr. Sheets's condo would be available the weekend of March 12. It would be just before Iris was to visit Israel.

She had been busy during February getting gifts for her family when not occupied with printing and framing photos for the display at the mall. On my coming home the evening the exhibit opened, Iris accosted me at the door.

"Bob, I have so much to tell you. First, guess who come to our school to give talk?"

"I don't know, but if it isn't blond, female, and buxom, I'm not interested."

Iris was in too much of a hurry to laugh. She took hold of my arm. "Oh, you big jerk. Listen, Arthur Rothstein come. He big and famous photographer and he coming to our school. I able to show him my pictures and he will comment on them. I so excited. And we must go to the mall to see my pictures, they up and I no wait to see them." Placing her head on my shoulder she gently chewed on my ear before whispering: "You know it soon be our anniversary too, and I need new camera."

I pulled back, wiping my ear dry. "What's wrong with the old camera?"

Iris went back to chewing and whispering in my ear. "Well, it okay but it not good for professional photography. Bill say I need two-and-a-half-inch format, that thirty-five millimeter not good for big pictures. Now you see how good my work is, don't you want it to be better?"

I stood for a second in silence as she tickled my ear with her tongue and continued trying to convince me. "Besides, it not really that much. Don't you think that be nice present for anniversary? Think that my birthday come up in July, then you maybe get gold necklace for me or—"

"Okay, okay, I surrender. You can get the camera," I said, as my ear was getting waterlogged. I pulled back.

Iris held on to me, kissed me, and laughed. "You see Bob, Israeli women much smarter than American men. Now let's eat so we can go to mall and see my pictures."

We arrived at the mall and looked at the pictures from her class. Iris went down the line critiquing each work. Suddenly she stood mesmerized in front of a group of photos. Her sudden silence and radiant face made me think she had seen the Messiah.

Still transfixed, she said softly, "These are mine."

I really did feel that each photo expressed a story. The one of her mother looking up, waving a cigarette, so matter-of-fact, taken during her visit to us. It showed a woman confident and calm. The one of a young cowboy approaching, mouth partially open, about to speak. I looked at it, expecting him to say something to me. I thought to myself you could teach someone about lighting and filters, but you couldn't tell someone when to press the shutter, when the picture transformed from a photo to a story. Iris seemed to have that gift. I was immensely proud that she had come so far and had such talent.

A few weeks later Arthur Rothstein came to Odessa. Iris presented her photos to him. "He say picture of my mother very good but he didn't like the children in the video game. I thought he say better things but it seem he not say very much good to anyone. Bob, he give talk on March 12. I want that we go. What you say?"

The talk was the night before we were to leave for Ruidoso, but I felt that would not be a problem and gladly agreed to go. There was to be a party reception after, and it sounded like it would be an enjoyable evening. However, that was two weeks away.

The next morning I was off to work and an evening medical meeting. I arrived home before Iris as Iris was busy developing pictures at school. Arriving home soon after, she dropped her books on the sofa.

"I exhausted. I think I go to bed right away. How your day?"

"Oh, pretty good. My patients are still alive, and no one is threatening to sue me, so I guess I bluffed my way through another day. By the way, I thought you were done with your developing for this semester."

"No, I still have portfolio to do. I not think I get it ready, but Bill say I can take pictures in Israel and use. I think I have so much to do before I go to Israel that I never finish in time. Maybe we not go to Ruidoso next week," she said, going to the bedroom to change.

I followed, placing my hands around her waist. "A little rest will do you good. Besides, I want to take you skiing, or that is watch you ski while I, the fearless leader that I am, hide in the ski lodge just in case you need medical assistance."

"Oh, Bob, you crazy," she said pulling my hands away and starting to undress.

I watched as she changed. Her form was perfect except for the legs. Why so scarred with veins? I thought. It just didn't make sense, such a beautiful woman with the legs of an old lady.

"Bob, tell me that you love me. Tell me." Her hands enveloped around my neck.

"Iris, I love you this much," I said as I spread my arms out, imitating a bird's wings. "And if my arms were longer, I would love you that much more."

Iris released her hold on me and got into bed. She pulled up the covers and became more serious "Bob, I have important things to discuss with you. I call my family. They say they find doctor for me that fix my legs. It new procedure, but he make all the lines go away. Then I look pretty. What you think?"

I thought she had somehow read my mind, but I didn't want her to do anything foolish. I asked her about the qualifications of the doctor, and I told her I thought she was pretty. I climbed into bed beside her and nuzzled my nose between her breasts.

Iris shouted, "Stop it, you maniac." In a softer tone she went on: "Now listen. My mother says friends of her have had it done with good results. I think I go to the doctor when I in Israel and see. Besides, you say I'm pretty when you don't mean it. You think I not pretty and I think—"

I came up for air to interrupt her, "I think you shouldn't think so much. Now hear this. You are a very desirable woman and no matter what your legs look like there is beauty in your face and the curve of your figure not to mention the maturity of your mind. I don't want to hear you degrade yourself. I think, or rather I know, you are beautiful and that is all. Now, do you understand?"

Iris smiled as she leaned forward to kiss me.

"What else did your mother say?" I asked.

"She send her regards to you and hope all is well. She sorry that you not able to come. Oh Bob, I so excited I no able to sleep at night thinking about going home. I go see all my friends and go to army base and see all the people I know. And I see Alina and Noah. Alina need some advice on her boyfriends. And I see my grandfather and grandmother. I no believe that I not home for a year. Oh Bob, I look so forward to it. Now you remember not to be alone on Passover and I call you every day to be sure you all right." She rolled on top of me and started to kiss me.

"Every day, every day you call?" I blurted out above her lips.

"Oh, be quiet," she said recovering my lips as we made love and went to sleep.

All is good!

CHAPTER FIFTY
On Her Own

The next few days passed quickly as Iris went about getting her portfolio ready for school and buying and packing gifts for Israel.

It wasn't long before it was time for the Rothstein lecture. I arrived at the college that evening. The event was held at the college auditorium. In the lobby outside the entrance to the auditorium Iris was talking to a couple. There were hors d' oeuvres being served and cocktails. She looked so relaxed, leaning on one leg and waving a wineglass in the air.

"I glad you here. This is Bob, my husband. This Sally and her husband Jim," Iris said, shifting her drink to the other hand and hooking her arm around mine.

I shook hands with Sally and Jim, and as the lecture was to begin, the cocktail glasses were put aside as we entered the hall. The lights dimmed as we found a couple of seats. The speaker, a sprightly gentleman, took the podium. It was hard to believe this man was showing pictures he had taken fifty years before. It seemed he should be dead, not looking like he was just starting his career. The pictures rolled by of migrant workers, presidents, movie stars. It was history with an artistic brush.

"And when I started," said Mr. Rothstein, "the government was the only one providing jobs. Here is a picture of me when I was nineteen, starting out on one of my first assignments under the National Recovery Act. You can see that my equipment was modest—just a camera and tripod. This is one of my most famous photos, of the father and son returning to their shack in a dust storm. It is one of the most iconic pictures of the Depression era. Here is a picture of the son taken a few years ago. I still keep up with the family. The next picture, of the skull in the desert, is . . ."

For my part I could not get over the fact that the man who had shot these old Depression-era pictures from the 1930s was standing in front of me in Odessa, Texas, in 1982. He went on to talk about his new projects, teaching, and future plans. It made me think of my own life.

Will I be so productive and accomplish so much? Will I continue to grow and seek out new challenges, as Rothstein did? Or will I just be complacent in doing the same thing every day, never widening my interests or accomplishments? Will I be the man on the stage or the man in the audience?

Iris listened quietly, nodding at times in agreement. Her eyes never once in two hours drifted from the speaker. When it was over, she exhaled deeply, as if this was her first breath of the evening.

Exiting the hall, she commented: "Oh, wasn't it wonderful that he able to do so much? His work is very good. You know, I want to get his autograph."

We followed the crowd out of the auditorium back to the lobby. As the lobby filled, Iris's teacher, Bill, was calling for order. "Attention, attention. I've got a few awards I'd like to make before we get into socializing. You will all have a chance to talk to our distinguished guest, but first, a little business. I have several scholarships to present from Odessa College for next semester. These are given to those people who have proven to have outstanding abilities. The first goes to Sally Newton"

Sally, a young woman, blushed as she came forward to receive her award.

"Congratulations, Sally." Bill shook her hand.

Iris clapped. "She is so nice, and her work very good."

Next was Mark Fielding, who came forward to receive his award.

Iris turned toward me. "Mark been doing it much longer than me, but I think my work better."

"And the last award goes to Iris Jaffee," Bill announced.

Iris who? My wife winning a college award?

Iris was all smiles. She gave me a kiss on the forehead and went to receive her certificate. Standing straight, beaming, she shook Bill's hand and took the award.

"Iris, did you know that you were going to get this tonight?" I asked as I read the certificate. It was a voucher for free tuition for next semester.

"No, I very surprised," she said. "Isn't it wonderful? This means that my work is good. I think it be better with practice." Her face could have lit the room with the lights out. "Well, why don't you kiss me? Don't you think it good?"

"Oh, why. of course, it's terrific," I said placing a small kiss to her lips. "I'm very proud. I never got anything like this. Most of the schools I went to just wanted me to leave as soon as possible."

Iris laughed.

I was my usual sarcastic self. "If you don't go back to school next semester, do you think we can trade this award in for dinner or something?"

"Bob, hush up. This big honor. Come with me. I want you to meet Julie and her husband."

"Hello, Iris. Wasn't the talk wonderful?" Julie said, reaching out to touch Iris's arm. Julie looked to be in her forties, slender, and elegantly dressed.

"Oh, I enjoy it so much," Iris said, looking directly into Julie's eyes.

"And congratulations on your award," Julie added, giving Iris a hug.

I was amazed that Iris got along on an equal footing with people old enough to be her parents.

"I so surprised. I never expect this happen," Iris said as she saw something that caught her attention. "Oh, there Mr. Rothstein. I want to get his autograph. I be right back." She found a large poster advertising his lecture on the wall, took it down, and brought it over for him to sign.

"Dr. Jaffee," Julie continued. "You must be so proud of your wife. I can tell you she certainly tires me out. We go out to take pictures and she never has enough. And so imaginative too. Even though I'm so much older than Iris, I look forward to seeing her in class. She is so full of enthusiasm, and she speaks so highly of you."

I grinned as if I was receiving the award. Iris came running back to show us the autograph, and we talked with Julie for another minute before talking to other acquaintances. Not knowing anything about photography, I stood in the corner for the rest of the evening, talking to an empty glass of wine and a piece of cheese. I watched as Iris would smile, wave, shake hands, laugh, and get into serious conversations.

She has made friends and found her interest. I may have enough degrees to paper the wall, but I could never do what she has accomplished, learning a foreign language, taking up photography, adjusting to a different culture, all while far away from family and Israeli friends. She is amazing.

I smiled again to myself.

She has had to contend with me, a demanding, not always sympathetic husband. She doesn't resemble the person who used to nap on the sofa, waiting for her husband to return home from work. I am not going to dominate our relationship. We are equals. Probably the only thing I can beat her at is math.

No, I don't think I have anything to worry about. She will come back from Israel. She is a success. Like a rosebush in winter, the thorns of despair and insecurity have weathered the season to a flowering summer of confidence and happiness.

* * *

As we lay in bed that evening, Iris had an idea. "You know, Bob, that Mr. Rothstein very interesting man. You know he have relatives in Israel, and I tell him that I be happy to take message to them. He give me address."

I was surprised that she would want to spend some of her vacation time tracking down Rothstein's relatives, but Iris had an answer.

She looked at me with a devilish smile. "Well, you know his relative will want to say something to him in the States and so when I go back to States and visit in New York where he live, I bring back messages. I also bring my pictures. You think he mind looking at my work while I tell him about his relatives?" Her smile grew wider and wider as it dimpled her cheeks.

I started to laugh. I could not believe my young wife had become so devious. She had such street sense. I turned out the lights and settled myself for sleep, but almost immediately felt a blow to my back.

"What's the matter with you that you no kiss me and hold me? Is this night different?" Iris said, continuing to knock on my shoulders.

I turned to honor her request.

"Oh, Bob, I so happy," she said as she began to fall asleep.

I held her until our joyful tears had dried.

CHAPTER FIFTY-ONE
Ruidoso

*I*t was a long drive to Ruidoso, and I was running late in the office. I called Iris at home. "Get everything ready; I'll be home about five thirty. Tell Avi and Carmella to meet us at our apartment." I rushed through the last patients, jumped into the car and drove home.

The living room greeted me with enough equipment for a trip to Mt. Everest.

"Iris, where the hell do you think we are going? Do we really need all this photographic stuff? I'm taking you skiing, not to a photo fair," I said peering down at the floor. "Look at this, two cameras, three lenses, a tripod, two bags of other junk. Where am I supposed to sit in the car? Now really, Iris, a tripod? What are you going to do, mount it on a ski?"

"Now, Bob, you remember what Mr. Rothstein say he start with?"

"Yeah, a camera and a tripod, but—"

"So, you see that absolutely necessary. Now be a good husband and bring to car."

I gathered as much equipment as I could carry. "If Mr. Rothstein owned all this stuff when he started, he would have opened up a store, sold it, and retired."

"You hush. You want to be in way of me being famous photographer?" She saw me drop one of the lenses and screamed, "Now be careful!"

Avi and Carmella arrived while I was loading the vehicle, a large BMW sedan Dr. Sheets had given me. I jokingly told them to get in the car before all the space was taken by Iris's equipment.

"Bob, not to worry. There plenty of room, let me arrange it," Avi said, helping me place the belongings in the trunk. "Carmella and I really look forward to this. I hope we get to go skiing. I never get chance to try in Israel. You know they have one ski place in Israel, near Syria. Maybe I be expert and be teacher there."

As for me, I had tried skiing in the past and discovered trees were harder than my head. "You can all go skiing and I'll stay in the lodge."

Iris watched, supervising the packing. "Bob, you change mind about skiing."

"No, when you're as old and clumsy as me, it's time to retire. Besides, I tried skiing. I was pretty good getting down the hill, I just couldn't figure out how to stop. That was until I met the tree." I took a deep sigh. "Oh, to be young again."

"Oh Bob, you not that old, you just act it," Iris said, pleased that her gear was safely aboard.

Carmella handed me a white bag. "I made some sandwiches, in case we get hungry,"

"Well, let's get going," I said, as the rest of the suitcases were thrown into the car.

Two hours into the five-hour trip we stopped in Pecos to eat Carmella's sandwiches. We found a vacant gas station in town. It was 11:00 p.m., and everything in the town was closed. There was just quiet: no people, and except for an occasional car, no traffic. We ate sitting on the curb at the vacant gas station, chewing in the semidarkness with just the faint glow from an overhead streetlight. The night was clear, the temperature in the forties, with a mild breeze.

"Oh, I think this is going to be so much fun," Carmella said.

"Dr. Sheets have a very big place we stay at with pool table and kitchen and lots of bedrooms with fireplace. It very nice," Iris said, as she ate with one hand and held onto my arm with the other.

"Well, I show you all that there nothing to this skiing," Avi boasted as he passed around the thermos.

"Well, we will never know what a great skier you are Avi unless we get to Ruidoso so let's get going," I said as I and the rest finished eating.

When Carmella and Avi started back to the car, Iris turned to me. "Bob, maybe you take some marijuana so you be better in bed."

"Huh? What? I was always good enough for every one of my other girlfriends," I said semi-truthfully.

Iris looked at me sympathetically. "Maybe you change and need some help." She smiled and kissed me on the lips. "Oh, I so excited. In just two weeks I be back in Israel. It seem like dream," Iris said as we started to get up and go back to the car.

Iris leaned her head on my shoulder as we walked. "I love you," she whispered.

I took her head between my hands and looked directly at her. "I must be the luckiest man in the world to have you," I said, giving her a kiss as we climbed into the car.

I had done the driving up to this point. It was late and I had risen early and worked the entire day. I must have looked the way I felt: worn out.

"Bob, you tired. I drive," Avi said.

Iris and Carmella took the backseats. I got into the front passenger's seat as Avi took the wheel, and we were off again.

"Oh, I wish I go with you to Israel," Carmella said. "You will have room to take back some mail for me?"

"Of course," Iris responded.

Avi started to sing some Israeli songs, and Carmella and Iris joined in, while I listened.

"Bob, join in," Avi commanded.

"It easy," Carmella said as she slowed down the tempo for me to grasp a phrase.

"I'll just hum," I said as it became obvious I wasn't going to be able to sing in Hebrew. The night was clear with stars everywhere. We opened the sunroof and let the sounds of Israeli songs fill the empty air to the heavens.

In a brief time the singing stopped. I turned to see Iris sleeping in the back seat behind Avi, with her head against the window. Carmella, beside her, also started to fall asleep. I settled in my seat beside Avi and soon joined Iris and Carmella in repose. Everything seemed so peaceful, so perfect. On a barren road, on a clear night, I could never have predicted how the next hour would change it all.

CHAPTER FIFTY-TWO
A Week Away

"Oh, my God, oh, my God! We've been hit! Oh, my God, I couldn't get out of way," Avi screamed.

Before I could grasp what was happening, the car came to a stop. No lights in the blackness, and for an infinite second, no sound.

What happened? Did we hit a tree? Did Avi fall asleep and lose control of the car?

"Oh, my God, he came right at us. What could I do? What could I do?" The only sound was Avi's wailing. The blackness covered everything. There was no immediate clue to anything more than we had run off the road.

From the backseat came Carmella's shaking voice: "What happened?"

"Are you all right?" I asked reflexively, turning toward the backseat.

"Yes, I think so," Carmella said haltingly.

I turned my head toward Avi to ask the same question.

"Yes Bob, I'm okay. I couldn't get out of the way," Avi said continuing the conversation with himself.

I again turned to the backseat. "Iris, are you okay?" I called, still trying to make out any objects in the darkness. There was no sound; the darkness revealed nothing. I got out of the car and opened Carmella's rear door. She stepped out holding her stomach, placing her hand on my shoulder for support. We took a few steps around the car to the driver's side.

"I'm okay, I'm okay," Carmella said as Avi got out and put his arm around his wife to guide her away from the vehicle.

"You all right? Are you all right?" I heard him asking her.

Why isn't Iris saying anything?

"Iris, are you okay? Iris, say something." I said as I opened her door and probed the darkness of the backseat.

So dark—it's so dark.

Nothing but a bit of moonlight for illumination. My hands groped along, feeling bits and pieces of shattered glass on the seat. I felt until I my fingers touched what I knew was some hair and a head and face. I pulled Iris's form toward me across the seat to bring her closer to the moonlight. There was no resistance. My fingers came away from her hair covered with a honeylike stickiness. I took hold of her torso and moved her out of the car into the moonlight and laid her on the ground.

"Iris, are you all right? Iris, say something. Are you all right?" I was so impatient for an answer, my words ran into each other leaving my mouth.

Silence, just silence. But then there was a movement of the lips.

"What, Iris? What? I can't hear you. No don't speak, don't talk."

*What to do? What to do? Relax, get hold of yourself. Remember, you're a doctor. Airway, breath, circulation. Yes, yes, check the airway to make sure it's not obstructe*d.

I turned Iris onto her right side, opened her mouth and swept around it with my fingers. *Get her tongue out of the way,* I told myself as I pulled her tongue down.

Don't let her aspirate. Keep her head to the side.

My fingers held the left side of her head for stability. But there was something wrong. It was so wet, her face so irregular feeling.

What is this?

I moved my body to allow the bit of moonlight to illuminate Iris's face.

"Oh, my God, oh, my God." The blond hair was now matted together from the drying liquid, black in the darkness. My fingers could feel the indentation of her skull better than my eyes could see in the dim light. There were jagged bits of bone and flesh, but I could not visualize anything clearly. For a fraction of a second, I pictured her as the beautiful woman she was, standing before a mirror, turning to and fro to be sure all angles were equally pretty—now so disfigured.

Hell, would she even want to survive? What a stupid thought. Don't even think something so stupid. Do something. What should I do? My wife is dying. Tell me what I should do?

Her mouth again opened and closed each time, letting out more dark liquid.

Blood—this is blood—blood everywhere.

"Iris, what? Oh, God, Iris, I love you so much, don't go. Please don't go," I said.

She's dying. Oh, my God, she's dying.

"No, Iris, don't go," I repeated, moving the hair back away from her face. Black, sticky liquid was everywhere.

She would be terribly upset knowing her hair was like this. She would never tolerate her long blond hair, her pride, being so disheveled.

Then her mouth stopped moving.

"Iris, say something. Iris, say something. I love you. Don't go. Don't leave me," I demanded in the silence and darkness.

Feel for a pulse; she's probably unconscious.

No pulse.

"Bob, how is she?" came Avi's voice from the darkness.

"Avi, she may be dead," I said, a twenty-year-old girl—no, my woman—quiet as if asleep in my arms.

"No, it's not true, I'll stop somebody. We'll get help, it's not true," Avi loudly protested as he turned and walked up the embankment. "Help, somebody help!" he yelled.

I looked at Iris, who was unmoving, her mouth still. I pulled my fingers away from where they were glued to her hair by the congealed blood.

"Oh, God, oh, God," I whispered to myself. "Maybe I'm wrong. Maybe she's not dead."

"I've got someone, I've got someone," Avi yelled, returning to where I knelt over Iris. "Bob, it won't be long now. They are calling for help. She'll be okay. Help will be here soon."

I tilted Iris's head back carefully where she lay on the ground.

I was scared. After so many years of training, I sat out there without the slightest idea of how to save my own wife. I just didn't know what to do. I had been sleeping a few minutes earlier. Now, looking down at my wife's lifeless body, on a deserted strip of road, I was trying to put together what was happening. I could not think straight, not about CPR, not about being a doctor. I wanted to just yell and run away as if that would make this all disappear.

Just above us, up the hill we were on, shone the headlights of a truck that had stopped—the driver who Avi said was calling for help.

Avi yelled, "Bob, she will be all right, she will be all right?"

"Maybe, Avi, I don't know," I heard myself say.

I don't believe this is real. This must be a bad dream.

Between the shouts coming from Avi and the others, there was just the quite broken by a few insect sounds. It was the type of lovely, cool evening when you closed your eyes and planned dreams; it was not the background for a nightmare. And yet here lay my wife, her skin pale in the weak moonlight.

"Avi, what happened?" I shouted.

"The car over there came from the opposite direction and just hit the rear of our car, where Iris sit. I better go and see if the driver is okay. You sure you all right?"

"Yes, I'm fine. You and Carmella, how about you?"

"I not hurt, but I think Carmella hurt pretty bad. She just stands there holding stomach. Bob, I be back in a second," Avi said, retreating.

It was so quiet and strangely peaceful, if not for our accident. The hazard lights of a truck blinked on and off rhythmically. "What can I do? What can I do?" I said over and over to myself as Carmella appeared from the shadows.

"How's Iris?" she asked.

"Very badly hurt. I don't think she is going to make it." It came out of me so softly, so matter-of-fact.

What is wrong with me? This is not another patient in the hospital. Not another conclusion after reviewing the chart. This is Iris. This is my wife. The end of a life that followed me halfway around the world, to stay and live with me and love me. Is that all I can say?

I wanted to do something to show my anger and sadness, but I was silent.

Maybe she isn't dead, maybe she will be all right.

"Carmella, are you all right?" I asked.

"I have a pain in my stomach, but I think I will be all right," she said. "I was asleep and didn't see anything." She grasped her stomach and bent over.

Avi's angry voice came out of the darkness. "That son of a bitch. I ask him if he okay and need help, and he just tell me to go away and leave him alone. The son of a bitch."

"Do you think he's hurt?" I asked.

"I don't know, but he didn't look hurt. Where are they? I wish they'd hurry," Avi said, turning away and looking down the road for an ambulance.

"Why don't you take care of Carmella? I will stay here with Iris," I told him as he took Carmella by the hand and led her away. I remained by the broken car with my silent wife.

Why the hell is she just lying here?

I didn't want Avi and Carmella to leave. I didn't want to be alone. But, no, better to be alone here, just the two of us. The two of us—yes, that was the way we had wanted it always.

What can I do? I think there is nothing left.

Her hair felt like a mat of straw. This was not the Iris I remembered. Her mouth was now half open but still. Maybe she had been trying to tell me something. I don't know. I took off my sweater and placed it over her chest. She was dressed in a sweatshirt, which could not be very warm in the chill breeze. As I placed the sweater over her, I could feel the wetness of her blood.

Where the hell are they? She can't possibly have any chance of surviving bleeding like this.

I spread the sweater out to cover as much of her as possible. Funny, I had never realized how delicate she was. Her shoulders so thin, bones so small.

"Iris, you are quite a lady—so dainty, a real lady. Iris you are my lady and I love you," I said, putting my arm around her to give her a little more warmth. Nothing I saw was the woman I remembered. Her broken face had no resemblance to the beauty that was once whole. I did not want to see her like this. I looked toward the blinking lights. Holding her, I could not believe what was on my mind—to even catch glimpses of the truth was a hell I didn't want.

When the ambulance arrived, I just waited by her side.

Now we have some help. Maybe I just missed the pulse. Maybe some IV fluids will restore it. She may only be in shock.

"Come with us. Come on," said the paramedic as he grasped me around the shoulders, lifting me up.

"But what about my wife? I can't leave her. She's . . . my wife. I just can't leave," I implored.

The paramedic pulled me along. "She'll be all right. We will take care of her. You can't do anything more."

"But I'm a doctor and I'm her husband," I shouted.

"Yes, yes, come along. We'll take her also, come along," the paramedic said dryly.

I followed him up to the ambulance. Looking over my shoulder I could see several shadows bending down over Iris. I climbed into the back of the ambulance, focusing my eyes as long as possible on the shadows by the car. The ambulance doors remained open for a minute. Avi and Carmella were already in the ambulance. An IV had been started on Carmella.

"Go ahead," came a shout from the destroyed car. The doors of the ambulance closed. I looked out the window into the darkness, staring at where the BMW was parked. Carmella was on a stretcher moaning softly. Avi knelt by her side, holding her hand and giving her encouragement. As it pulled away, I just looked out the back window of the ambulance, watching as the outline of the BMW quickly disappeared. I couldn't believe I was leaving my wife behind.

It just couldn't be, it just couldn't.

I brought my hand to my face and started to cry. It finally dawned on me, Iris was dead.

When we reached the hospital, Carmella was taken to an exam room where the doctor soon hospitalized her with a ruptured spleen. Avi and I had only some bruises and didn't need medical attention.

In the emergency room they brought in the driver of the other car. For a moment I caught a glimpse of him as he entered an exam room. He seemed fine. I didn't know what to think of him. Avi had told me that he aimed his can at ours, but I didn't know if this was true or if Avi had just fallen asleep at the wheel. I didn't care. Iris was dead. What difference did it make who was at fault?

I called Steven; I needed someone to talk to. I don't remember what I said, I needed someone to tell me what to do. I felt like was an actor who had forgotten his lines and was just standing alone on the stage.

"Have you notified Iris's parents?" he asked. "You must do this right away."

I did not know how I could possibly tell them. They were waiting for Iris to return home in two weeks. How was I to tell them she was dead? I didn't want to imagine how devastating this news would be.

* * *

After the call to Steven, I stood wishing I was the one killed in the accident. I just could not call Iris's parents, I just couldn't. But I had to. It had to be done and it was best that me, her husband, the one who took her to the US, should be the one to make the call. The longer I waited and thought the harder it would be. *Just do it! It must be done.*

I told myself. I listened to the ringing on the long-distance line. Ziggy picked up on the other end: "Bob, how are you?"

I didn't want to start crying. I closed my eyes and blurted out, "Ziggy, we have been in a terrible car accident. Iris is dead." I put the phone down as tears started flowing down my face. When I regained composure and placed the phone to my ear there was only silence.

After what seemed like hours Ziggy responded calmly. "You will bring her to Israel, okay?"

"Yes, yes, of course," I said softly and hung up.

* * *

Dr. Sheets sent his private plane to bring me, and Iris's remains back to Odessa. Avi stayed with Carmella at the hospital in Ruidoso. *No, no, this really didn't happen.* I told myself as I sat alone on the plane and looked out the window. I turned away from the window, placed my head in my hands and cried.

Steven came to Odessa, thank God, to help me. I didn't ask him, but I was unable to function, and he must have known it from our subsequent phone conversations. I remember standing in front of the closed funeral home, at night, and calling Iris's name. Steven, before he went back to Monticello, had to make the arrangements for the transfer of Iris to Israel, get me a plane ticket to Israel and take me to the airport. As the plane landed in Tel-Aviv the vibrant Israeli music came over the loudspeakers. I thought how different it sounded in my ears from the first time of excitement and dreams of everlasting happiness had now turned into a funeral dirge.

* * *

I stood in a cemetery by the sea, loose, sandy soil blowing in the wind. Wispy clouds punctuated the blue sky. The sun was pleasantly warm.

Why such a beautiful day for such a terrible event?

I saw Ziggy in a suit, stoic, standing silently. Sarah was too emotionally affected to come. I reached out to touch the shroud, to feel the form of the woman I loved. The slender shape was without change. The physical heat of life replaced by the emotional warmth of memory.

I listened to the rabbi speak in Hebrew—the same seventy-year-old rabbi who had married us but one year before. My hand held on to Iris's arm a little longer, a little longer to be with her. I thought of how I didn't kiss her in the supermarket, in the office, in the airport. Why didn't I show her the same affection she showered on me? Why didn't I spend more time helping and being with her? Why did I not always treat her as my equal? What made me think my job and diplomas made me better and more important than her? What good did it do now, to tell her how much I loved her, how much I admired all she had accomplished in the short year we were married? What good now, to tell her how wrong my ideas of marriage were? As the prayers were recited, I could only stand in silence.

What is left, what remains? The years will find no monuments, no holidays, no celebrations for this young woman—only my memories of her love, determination, and courage. Those are my only keepsakes.

Slowly Iris was lowered into the ground. Someone reached out and grabbed my arm, pulling me back as they began to shovel Iris's eternal blanket of earth over her.

* * *

At the Tel Aviv airport, as I made my return to Odessa, I remembered that photo of Iris when I left her behind the first time I visited her in Israel. I remembered the rainy day, the sad expression, the tall, beautiful woman in the oversized crimson coat, standing alone, wondering if her Bob would ever return.

And now her Bob was leaving her behind forever.

Iris returns to Israel, forever.

EPILOGUE

*I*ris was killed by a driver who was trying to commit suicide and purposely aimed his car at our vehicle. He lived; Iris died. He was told by the police to return at once to his home in California and avoid any further responsibility. Was this God's will? What faultless God takes the life of the innocent? How can I accept what I can't explain? I want to perpetuate the life of Iris. But only in memories does she exist, and with their passing, she is forgotten—just another headstone among endless rows of headstones. The sweet memories of what was are bitter consolation for what should have been. I cannot look in perpetuity for answers that don't exist. I must accept tragedy as an essential part of life. But coping doesn't mean forgetting, doesn't mean the grief has passed or the memory gone. Memories live in the present, waiting to be ignited by a word, an object, or just a moment of solitude. The loss is never left behind.

When I returned to Texas after the funeral, I filled a room with Iris's photos: the ones she took and the photos of her. Every evening I would talk to these photos, but they were always silent. Her spirit remained, but so sorely missed was her bodily presence. I thought of what she had said about going into practice with Steven. It would have been like Snow White taking a bite of the poison apple.

I did not stay in Texas; there were too many memories there.

Returning to New York, I started a successful solo ophthalmology practice, which I ran for thirty-five years. I wanted to stay in contact with Iris's parents so that I could talk about Iris. Just hearing her name made it seem as if she were still alive. But Sarah could see what I didn't: that life moves on. She encouraged me to go out, to get away from the room with all the photos.

I started to date and eventually remarried and started a family. It wasn't fair to bring Iris's memory into this new relationship, but I knew I had changed. Now I would reach across the table at a busy restaurant and kiss my wife. In my head was Iris's voice, echoing, "Who cares?" My hobby collecting Civil War memorabilia continued, but not in the bathroom. I can't say I have developed a love of shakshuka, but I have learned to do most of the cooking, clean the dishes, and smile. The attention, compassion, and respect I once held in reserve I now freely give in my marriage. Why wait until tomorrow to show

how much you love another, when tomorrow may never arrive? Iris never waited for tomorrow.

It has been forty years since that terrible day, but it never seems to be in the past.

In a corner of my attic lies a deteriorating leather camera bag. Inside the bag is Iris's camera with a roll of film ready to take pictures of an upcoming ski trip. In the silent corners of my mind I see a young woman with long blond hair, freckles, and boundless enthusiasm reaching for that camera. And so, I check that camera every week to see if the film has been advanced. I cling to the forlorn hope that one day that young woman will return.